WHEN
BETTER
ISN'T ENOUGH

WHEN BETTER ISN'T ENOUGH

EVALUATION
TOOLS FOR THE
21ST-CENTURY
CHURCH

Jill M. Hudson

THE
ALBAN
INSTITUTE

Herndon, Virginia

www.alban.org

Library of Congress Cataloging-in-Publication Data

Hudson, Jill M.
    When better isn't enough : evaluation tools for the 21st-century church /
    Jill M. Hudson.
        p. cm.
    Includes bibliographical references.
    ISBN 1-56699-289-3 (pbk.)
    1. Clergy—Rating of. 2. Church officers—Rating of. I. Title.
BV4011.7.H83 2004
253'.028'7—dc22

                                                            2003027995

11   10   09   VG   4   5   6   7   8   9   10

CONTENTS

ACKNOWLEDGMENTS

I am grateful to the Presbytery of Whitewater Valley for once again allowing me to use my study-leave time for the completion of a book. It is a wonderful postmodern judicatory committed to excellence in everything it does! Special thanks go to Ruth Ann MacPherson and Kristy Quinn, who provided administrative support for this project.

The world is full of effective pastors who are diligently leading their congregations through this time of great change. Among them are the Rev. Michael Slaughter, pastor of Ginghamsburg United Methodist Church in Tipp City, Ohio; the Rev. Mike Foss, pastor of Prince of Peace Lutheran Church in Burnsville, Minnesota; and the Rev. Brian McLaren, pastor of Cedar Ridge Community Church in Spencerville, Maryland. The opportunity to interview each has been invaluable to my research.

I would also like to thank Carol Childress, director of information services for Leadership Network, who started me on my search for effective postmodern churches and pointed me to excellent resources. The Rev. Roy Oswald, senior consultant at the Alban Institute, provided a thoughtful interview and field-tested the "12 characteristics of an effective pastor" in his workshops. The Presbytery of Western Reserve assisted me in January 2003 with an invitation to meet with a group of pastors to discuss the model presented in this book.

I am indebted to these ministers and congregations that field-tested the process and the instruments found in Appendixes A and B:

The Rev. Elisabeth Baer and St. Peter's United Church of Christ. Evansville, Indiana.

The Rev. Judy Doll and the United Church of Christ congregations of St. Jacob's at Blue Creek and St. John's at Penntown in Sunman, Indiana.

The Rev. Harry Eberts III and Lyndhurst Community Presbyterian Church, Lyndhurst, Ohio.

The Rev. David Lee and Hopewell Presbyterian Church, Franklin, Indiana.

The Rev. John Lentz and Forest Hill Presbyterian Church, Cleveland, Ohio.

The Rev. Tom MacMillan and John Knox Presbyterian Church, North Olmsted, Ohio.

The Rev. Chuck McNeil and the Federated Church of Grass Lake, Grass Lake, Michigan.

The feedback of these pastors and congregations led to stronger and, I hope, more usable evaluation tools.

Most of what I know about the postmodern world I learned from my favorite teacher, my husband, Jay. His love of the church and fascination with the culture has been a constant source of creativity in our home. I am thankful to share both life and ministry with him. This book is dedicated to Jay Hudson and to pastors everywhere who work to make faith relevant and the church effective in this new age. To God be the glory!

FOREWORD

In the spring of 2003, *The Journal News,* a Gannett newspaper serving
Westchester, Rockland, and Putnam counties in New York, published
an article claiming that mainline Protestants are reeling.[1] Writer Gary
Stern cites several church executives as they reflect on the congregations under their care. Here is an excerpt:

> Scores of churches across greater New York that are part of the "mainline" Prot-
> estant tradition are now gasping for life. Aging congregations of only a few dozen
> people have become commonplace, presenting the possibility that many
> churches will close over the next decade or so.
>
> A *Journal News* review of the five most prominent mainline denominations
> shows that their membership in New York City and the surrounding suburbs
> has fallen by 45 percent since the heyday of 1960, when the spiritual descen-
> dants of Luther, Calvin and Wesley composed the white-bread religious main-
> stream.

The five denominations—the United Methodist Church, the Evangelical Lutheran Church in America, the Episcopal Church, the Presbyterian Church (U.S.A.) and the United Church of Christ—have been loath to close churches and sell off valuable real estate. As a result, they continue to operate more than 1,000 churches in the region for 300,000 members.

The Rev. James Vande Berg, head of Presbyterian Church (U.S.A.)'s Hudson River Presbytery, expects that half his churches could close in 10 to 20 years. He foresees a day when several mainline congregations in the Hudson Valley will share church buildings and perhaps ministers. Other leaders are less frank but predict that churches that do not change—and soon—will die.

Articles like this have appeared in numerous places under various headlines. Certain evangelical parachurch organizations even claim that all mainline Protestant churches will have disappeared within 20 years. *Personally, I don't believe a word of it.*

Church professionals who claim that mainline congregations are about to become extinct seem to think that all our clergy are dimwits who are stuck in the past. They assume our lay leaders are uncommitted Christians who will only accept a church that remains linked with traditional church music and formal worship. They don't believe we have what it takes to become "turn-around" congregations that are relevant to our postmodern era. What they are failing to see are the numerous vital and growing mainline congregations that are making a positive impact on their communities.

When I conduct a training event that involves mainline clergy, I usually begin with some exercises that use open-space technology. I ask people to walk to different parts of the assembly hall to show how they personally respond to certain questions. So I might instruct, "Those people who have remained in the denomination of their childhood, go to this side of the room; those having changed denominations in their lifetime, go to the opposite side of the room." One of the scenarios I set up is always this: "Those representing congregations that have grown in worship attendance over the past five years, go to that side of the room. If your congregation has maintained worship attendance over the past five years, stand in the middle of the room. Those whose congregations have experienced a decline in worship attendance over the past five years, move to the opposite side of the room." In every workshop where I have done this exercise, at least two-thirds of the group stands on the side of the room representing growth in worship attendance. About a quarter of the group is in the middle. Only a handful of the clergy stand on the side of the room representing a decline in worship attendance.

To be sure, clergy attending an Alban Institute training event do not represent your normal cross-section of clergy in any given denomination. These are people who are motivated to learn more about how to run an effective, growing congregation. Many of the clergy in declining congregations are not attending the kind of events Alban sponsors. There is no question in my mind, however, that many mainline congregations are growing in congregational participation. Unfortunately, mainline Protestant denominations are in decline because more *congregations* are in decline than are growing. But beware if you find yourself discounting any mainline denomination.

Will growing effective congregations be easy? Not by a long shot. In *When Better Isn't Enough*, Jill Hudson explodes two myths we find in many congregations. The first is that we can grow without changing. You might be surprised by how many congregations believe this. They want to continue to do the same old things but expect different results. Each year when they review their statistics, they shake their heads in bewilderment, not understanding why worship attendance and congregational participation has not grown.

The second myth congregations hold on to for dear life is that we can change without conflict. All we need to do is get together and develop a new strategic vision that will not upset anyone but will reverse our congregation's decline. When they do try some new things that might attract new members but that also upset some of current members, they quickly shut down the new plan, so as not to lose any longtime members. Nancy Ammerman's book *Congregation & Community* contains many examples of congregations that were in decline but made changes and reversed this trend.[2] Ammerman offers not one example of a congregation that turned around without one huge fight that resulted in some people leaving the congregation. *Not one single example!*

When Better Isn't Enough is classic Jill Hudson work. As you read this book, you will soon notice that what she has to say is not for the faint-hearted. You will also learn something about how to grow a congregation in a postmodern era. For years, Jill has served with me on the staff of Alban's 10-day Clergy Development Institute. For the past five years, she has been our specialist on congregational change and the realities that face congregations in a postmodern age. This part of the Institute is not easy on participants, some of whom wonder if they can make it to retirement before they have to deal with change in a postmodern era. Yet most participants come to embrace the new realities of our times and leave with some handles to begin or continue change within their congregations. I would consider it a real loss if Jill were no longer part of this Institute and the 30-plus participants who attend the event every year were to lose the insights she has gathered in this book.

Roy M. Oswald
Senior Consultant
The Alban Institute

IT'S A NEW DAY 1

A PLEASANTVILLE SUNDAY. THE ALARM CLOCK ALWAYS STARTLES
Bill, but he'd never dream of sleeping in. It's Sunday morning, and he has to make coffee for his wife, Mary, before waking the kids and starting the weekly ritual of preparing for church. Bill has taught the high-school church-school class for the past several years, and Mary sings in the choir. They always try to get to church early so that he can prepare his classroom. If Betty, their 15-year-old, can't decide which dress to wear, she can easily walk the three blocks and join them there. The boys—Sam, Bob, and Davy—are another story. They'll need to polish their shoes, review the memory verse for this week, and hope that Mom didn't forget to iron their dress shirts. Bill always allows an extra five minutes for the trip so that the boys can run back into the house to retrieve their forgotten offering money from their piggy banks. He wonders what the topic of this morning's message will be. Pastor Higgins sure delivers a powerful sermon! It gives the family plenty to talk about over the fried-chicken or pot-roast dinner Mary usually prepares on Sunday. Bill is employed by McHenry Insurance Company.

When Tom McHenry hired him almost 20 years ago, one of the first things he wanted to know was where Bill went to church. Bill and Mary are lifelong Methodists, growing up at St. Mark's in the youth group together. St. Mark's is an amazing congregation that has almost doubled its membership in the past 10 years. So many young families with children have joined that St. Mark's doesn't have room for everyone! The church board is planning a new addition to the educational wing. Bill and Mary belong to the couples club, which meets every other Friday night, and both serve on the benevolence committee. Bill is grateful that he no longer has to travel for his job, since his church involvement takes several evenings each week. He also picks up his widowed mother and takes her to Bible study on Wednesdays. Mrs. Miller finds great solace in her church, and that means a lot to Bill. She always spends Sunday afternoon with the family so they can return to church together for the evening service at 7:00. They'll probably pull out the Monopoly game again this week—maybe Bill will finally beat Davy, the family champion. The year is 1957. Life is good in Middle America.

Sunday in the City

This is the second time Kyle has slammed off the alarm. That darn snooze button! The clock reads almost 10, and Molly has been up for an hour. She always does her yoga on Sunday morning before they walk the dog down to the neighborhood bistro for brunch. There's nothing like the Sunday *New York Times,* a good omelet, and fresh-brewed decaf. Lying in bed, Kyle remembers the conversation he had with his co-worker Magritte on Friday afternoon. In talking about weekend plans Magritte mentioned that she'd be with her church group all day Saturday, helping to winterize the homes of some elderly people in a low-income neighborhood. Kyle had been impressed with her commitment. He'd been volunteering once a month at a citywide food pantry and found it rewarding. He always hated the thought of the long drive, and giving up a Saturday wasn't much fun; but he found himself talking to Molly about it for days afterward. Besides, community service looked good on a résumé. Kyle wondered what it might be like to work with a church group. He remembered being taken to Sunday school a few times as a child, but when his parents divorced, his mother quit going. Molly wasn't very interested in religion, having grown up in the Bible Belt, where so many biases and prejudices persisted. She had attended a Unitarian service a few times with a man she dated before she met Kyle. When planning their wedding, she turned to the Unitarian pastor to conduct the service. Kyle guessed he believed in a God, but he rarely gave much thought to it. Molly, on the other hand, was certain you weren't going to find God in a church. She believed, and was quick to tell you, that God dwells in the heart of each person. Church would be the last place to look for God. Being kind to people and working to be a "good" human being was the important thing for Molly.

On the other hand, Kyle realized that this was the third move they'd made since marrying. His position in computer design wasn't all that stable in the present economy. They didn't have a lot of friends. Maybe the church would be a place to connect with other couples their age. Lately, he'd been wondering if their routine was all there was to life. His Dad had just remarried for the fourth time; he and Molly were determined that divorce would never happen to them. They were saving for a down payment on a house so they could start a family, but he lived with the fear that his company might go belly up. How could they expect to raise a child with such uncertainty and no family nearby to help? Things were fairly confusing. Magritte seemed to be a peaceful person, not nearly as anxious about life as he was—and she and her husband had two small children at home. Maybe they were on to something. Perhaps he'll ask Magritte more about her church tomorrow. But for now, the bistro calls, and the paper is waiting. It's 2004 and life is—well, OK, in urban America.

A Time of Transition

These stories are not unfamiliar to many of us. We either lived them, or we watch as others live them now. Something has happened to our world, our culture, and the church. If you are over 50, you remember a time when Sunday morning was a community event. Almost everyone considered an upstanding citizen was in worship somewhere. Our nurseries overflowed, and we built and built—new sanctuaries, new educational wings—and when they were full, we started new congregations. Most Americans began and ended their professional life in one career, most marriages lasted "till death us do part," and life was fairly predictable. Today most people can expect to relocate several times and work for any number of companies. Second- and third-career choices are not unusual. College education is no longer the ticket to success. Individuals who attend worship one Sunday a month are now considered "active," and a whole generation of young adults has grown up without any religious background at all. Sunday is a day of recreation when one can easily see a movie, go to a game, or buy a car. What happened? How did this change come about? What in the world does this shift of eras have to do with a book on ministry evaluation?

Many sociologists and a growing number of church scholars are referring to the early 21st century as the transition from the modern era to the postmodern. Whenever a shift of this magnitude occurs, it leaves all of life, including the church, in flux. When anxious or insecure, people clutch desperately to the familiar. They strive to re-establish what has worked in the past. They want to stabilize the situation. As I teach and do consulting work across denominations, I find congregations that are longingly trying to return to the wonderful days of the 1950s. These church members, in good faith, believe their pastor and other staff could take them there by working harder at what had always worked before. Most congregations, when they take this posture, find themselves even more frustrated. The same old things done harder or better don't seem to make a difference. Depression about the state of the church sets in. Depression leads to conflict, and conflict leads to changes in leadership. Changes in leadership often leave congregations even less stable than before. How can we interrupt this cycle of disappointment? If the church in the 21st century wants to remain faithful, or even to survive, it must take a long, hard look at how we might bring the good news of Jesus Christ to a hurting, unstable, unpredictable, and often hostile world. We must identify new criteria for success, and perhaps even for faithfulness, and hold ourselves accountable to them, rather than measuring our effectiveness by criteria that were important in an earlier era of the world and church life. That's what this book is all about—looking at a new set of values by which we can measure effective ministry. We need, however, to understand the postmodern world before we can begin planning for the postmodern church.

A Look at the Postmodern World

"Postmodernism was born in St. Louis, Missouri, on July 15, 1972, at 3:32 PM."[1] It was at this moment the Pruitt-Igoe housing project, the epitome of modern architecture, was imploded. Designed to marry technology to the needs of society for the betterment of all, the project was a colossal failure. Residents vandalized the buildings, and despite numerous attempts by government to renovate the building and the concept behind it, officials finally gave up. Logically, one might believe that if people needed a place to live and the government would provide it, the problem could be solved to everyone's satisfaction. Obviously, that wasn't so. To Charles Jencks, famed postmodern architect, this event symbolized the death of the modern world, with its emphasis on science, logic, and reason; and the birth of postmodernity, in which conflicting beliefs can coexist, progress and knowledge aren't necessarily good, and people define truth from their personal experience.

The term *postmodernism* was coined in the 1930s, appearing on the fringes of society in the world of philosophy and literature.[2] In the 1960s architects and artists who hoped to offer an alternative to the predictable and functional offerings of the modern world adopted the term. The buildings of the time had been functional and practical—

but boring. Suddenly, it was fashionable to build a door going no-where—an attempt to stimulate the imagination and move beyond the obvious. By the 1970s this alternative way of viewing the world had become predominant in academia to describe the growing wave of social and cultural change; postmodernism has since become a defining word for today's popular culture. We see the word *postmodern* everywhere today—in business, in advertising, even in church. Postmodernism, however, is not just another phase or cycle, but a paradigm shift in its fullest definition—a movement between eras. It is of such magnitude that it reshapes how we think and will continue to think about life and our world for centuries to come.

In considering criteria for effective ministry in a postmodern era, we must first understand the dynamics of the world we're trying to reach. Contemporary writers have likened this time to the day Dorothy woke up in Oz. Mike Regele, author of *The Death of the Church*, describes it this way:

> For many of us, Kansas is a symbol of traditional America: a place where family is important and stability prevails, with good, hardworking people of the land—a secure place for children and adults. Kansas is an image of an era. The Land of Oz is a place of uncertainty where evil witches are at work. It is a place where things out of the ordinary occur. Where else do scarecrows talk and walk, are men made of tin, and do lions fail to be fierce and courageous? Oz is a place where things just are not the way they are supposed to be. It is an unstable place where the predictable is stood on its head.[3]

Evangelical scholar Stanley Grenz compares the TV series "Star Trek," a late-modern-era creation, with its new incarnation, "Star Trek—The Next Generation," as an illustration of the shift to postmodernism. The original series featured Spock, known to most readers as the part-human, part-Vulcan scientist with pointed ears, who used his dispassionate rationality to solve the problems encountered by the crew of the *Enterprise*. The new series features Data, an android who, though a rational machine capable of even greater problem-solving than Spock, believes that he's incomplete because he cannot understand what it means to be human with the ability to feel or dream. Religion, formerly ignored, takes on significance in the new, postmodern series with the introduction of a strange character, Q, who raises countless questions about the nature of divinity.[4] Whether we use Oz, the frontier of space, or the shattering awareness of how things have changed, we must admit the dramatic contrast between what was and what is rapidly unfolding in the world around us. In small towns and major cities all across America, modern and postmodern cultures do battle. No matter how hard we try, we all suspect that Humpty Dumpty can never be put back together again.[5]

Key Marks of the Postmodern World

Epistemology is the study of how we know things, how information comes into consciousness and becomes validated. The way human beings in today's world translate knowledge into "truth" is a primary key to understanding the shift to postmodernism. The modern era probably began around the dawn of the Enlightenment period (mid-1600s). The stage for it was set in the Renaissance with its emphasis on human accomplishment. Philosophers like René Descartes and scientists like Isaac Newton saw the physical world as one that could be mastered by the human mind. The focus of intellectual quest was to understand the universe so that it could be tamed for the betterment of humankind.[6] Moderns believed that knowledge is certain and that it can be objectively sought. They also believed that knowledge in and of itself is inherently good. The more we objectively know, the better off we are. This optimistic way of thinking was seen throughout the 20th century in humanity's desire to manage the world rationally. Technology and scientific discovery in all fields became the domain where truth could be known. In the 20th century progress was seen as inevitable if rooted in science and education. We could overcome nature, solve our problems, and rule our existence. The first glaring awareness that these assumptions might not be supportable came for many when the United States dropped two atomic bombs on Japan, hastening the end of World War II. We had mastered the technology, but at what price? The 1950s appeared to embrace the modern mentality to its fullest, but underneath the neat exteriors of life lay the gnawing possibility that perhaps things weren't quite what they seemed. The turbulent '60s lay the groundwork for postmodernism to rush fully into the consciousness of the 1970s. The women's movement challenged the right of white males to determine reality for both halves of the world's population! The Nixon-era Watergate scandal marked the loss of innocence for the American public, and trust in the integrity of politics began a downward slide. The scandals involving priests and pastors, which continue even today, shook the authority of religion in defining morality and embodying values. Deconstructionist approaches to history suddenly presented Christopher Columbus as an oppressor rather than a hero. "Negroes" became "blacks," then "African Americans," with the preferred term still in flux. We became aware that wild life was endangered along with the great forests and waters of the world. Where was truth, and who had the right to define it? Could anything other than one's own experience be trusted? Was all this so-called progress really bettering the world? Voilá!—postmodernism had fully arrived.

Over the past 30 years contemporary Western society has felt the tremors of change in ways that are both exciting and unsettling. The first truly postmodern generation was born after 1965. Many people of earlier generations who no longer believe that progress lies solely in technology also consider themselves postmodern. Today's world is composed of a blend of those who have never known anything other than a postmodern reality and those who still have a foot in both eras.

Postmodern reactions to the marriage of science and technology have had a wide-ranging effect. Quite often these are linked with "causes" such as the Green movement and its efforts to preserve the rain forests, ban animal testing, and cease production of genetically altered food. Science is no longer viewed as the only source of answers. More and more Americans are turning to alternative medicine, such as acupuncture, energy balancing, and herbal treatments. No longer are science and religion viewed as adversaries. Scientists are openly discussing the nature of God and the magnitude of the universe. The contributions of quantum physics have led many of the world's researchers to acknowledge that not everything can be measured by physical science.[7] Prayer has been recognized by physicians as an effective tool in the healing process. The postmodern world has a new appreciation for the mysterious, that which cannot be measured, contained, or quantified. We have validated a way of "knowing" that transcends the rational. No longer are the rules and principles that formerly governed society understood to be passed down through families, religious groups, or community norms. Morals, ethics, and values are created and re-created out of personal experience. Relationships become the crucible in which values are collaboratively constructed. There is a new renaissance in the search for principles, but postmoderns turn to one another to define them, not to sources outside their peer groups. Group-constructed values can be seen in the unspoken rules of the street gangs in Los Angeles and elsewhere, which form familylike bonds; in the lifestyle decisions of vegans; or in the convictions of members of the pro-life movement. One interesting survey revealed that four of every 10 individuals who were already involved in the Christian faith and active in a congregation in 2001 contended that there is no such thing as absolute moral truth.[8] The group is the most powerful shaper of the individual and of his or her beliefs.

Another important aspect of the postmodern world is choice— lots and lots of choice. The movement toward customization continues to grow. It has been possible for years to have a pair of denim jeans custom-tailored to fit you by simply following online ordering instructions. At the same time that the group is defining values and beliefs, the individual is shaping a particular identity. Anyone walking through an airport is no longer surprised to see a young woman of Generation X wearing a chiffon party skirt and black army boots. Think it's just the youth? Pick up a current copy of *Vogue*. Creating identity goes beyond what we wear. Last summer I taught a class in which one participant introduced herself as "Bob." When I encountered her sister later in the week, I discovered that her real name was Meredith but that she had enrolled under a pseudonym for the conference. For several decades some married couples have used hyphenated surnames to ensure that their individual identities are not compromised in marriage. Unlike their modern counterparts, postmoderns want to stand out, not fit in. The availability of choice is also an issue in the faith arena. People—those who have any religious background at all—no longer are typically baptized and buried in the same denomination. They pick and choose churches just as they might a car—by shopping around. This consumer mentality permeates religious life, as Alan Roxburgh, a Canadian author, points out: "Too many church leaders today feel like vendors of religious goods and services offering their wares to an army of hungry religious consumers who take, adapt, borrow, use, and discard the various aspects of Christian life as they pop in and out of our churches."[9]

It is the shifting approach to truth that likely has the greatest impact on the church. Postmoderns grant subjective experience as much weight in defining truth as they do objective fact. This inclination, in turn, leads to a socially constructed reality in which the "truth" of one's experience is far more important than fact or reason. Truth in the postmodern world is relative, and there are no absolutes. Actress Lily Tomlin, in her multifaceted performance in the one-woman play *In Search of Intelligent Life in the Universe*, sums this relativism up with a great line: "I can handle reality in small doses, but as a lifestyle it's much too confining."[10] One can hold multiple truths, even when they are contradictory. Someone can be a devout Methodist and still participate regularly in Native American spiritual practices; one can attend an Episcopal church and have a Buddhist altar in her home. In each case, a postmodern person will likely see no contradiction between deeply held Christian convictions and the practice of other religious traditions. A huge mark of the postmodern world is that one size does not fit all. Multiple stories coexist in the religious world; all of them may be viewed as having value. Postmodernism seems to be most evident when we observe what once might have seemed contradictory, such as a Buddhist Christian. We seem to live in an atmosphere of paradox that we no longer need to see resolved.[11]

Much more could be said about postmodernism, but these are the important points for a discussion about the church. The integration of rationality with imagination, intuition, and faith; the understanding that truth is socially constructed; and the ability to hold contradictory beliefs in tension are the primary keys for our continued discussion about what makes for effective ministry.

By the time you read this book, it will already be out of date. Such is the postmodern world—fast, changing, full of information, often brilliant, often frustrating. Readers over the age of 35 find themselves with a foot in two worlds, with much of their childhood and young adulthood still reflected in the modern world. Generations X, Y, and Z will always be more comfortable in the postmodern world than their elders will. Nevertheless, it is into this mix that we seek to bring the gospel of Jesus Christ, a 2,000-year-old story that is still relevant today.

THE CHURCH'S CHALLENGE: THE CHURCH IN THE POSTMODERN WORLD

2

> Postmodernism is a huge threat. Advocating the impossibility of knowing truth, it throws off all limits and casts us adrift in a sea of doubt.
>
> Postmodernism is a tremendous opportunity. It offers the potential for the rediscovery of spiritual reality and the integration of faith in everyday life.
>
> —Len Hjalmarson and Rob McAlpine, "Postmodern Possibilities"[1]

THESE TWO PERSPECTIVES PRETTY MUCH SUM UP THE GENERAL response by Christendom to postmodern reality. We either brace ourselves against the forces of change or embrace the opportunities that change provides. One thing we can agree upon—the church, like all contemporary institutions, is deeply affected by what is happening in our world.

I had the privilege of visiting in the office of Alban Institute founder Loren Mead in the early stages of his thinking about what would become his best-selling book *The Once and Future Church*. I remember his saying, "Jill, something really big is happening. I'm not sure what we'll do about it, but we've got to do something." This thinking, of course, led to his embracing the theory of the three eras of the church— the apostolic period of the early church, when the mission field was just beyond the doorstep; the long period of Christendom when church and state partnered in shaping the dominant culture of society; and the emerging era that Mead calls the "time between paradigms" and that I call the early postmodern era.[2] This time of uncertainty, excitement, chaos, and possibility is one that we dare not underestimate or write off as just another cycle in contemporary life. Mead was considered somewhat radical when, in 1991, he wrote, "We are at the front edges of the greatest transformation of the church that has occurred for 1,600 years. It is by far the greatest change that the church has ever experienced in America; it may eventually make the transformation of the Reformation look like a ripple in a pond."[3] He was not alone in his perspective. Donald Miller, professor of religion at the University of California, Los Angeles, wrote in his fascinating study of new-paradigm churches, *Reinventing American Protestantism*, "I believe we are witnessing a second reformation that is transforming the way Christianity will be experienced in the new millennium."[4] Canadian theologian Alan Roxburgh adds, "Make no mistake about it—every church leader must understand what has ended and be prepared for what is emerging if they are to lead God's people into and in the new century."[5]

Yet in many ways the church continues with business as usual, making plans as if we could will the 1950s back into existence. I share Mead's observation:

> I find many of my colleagues going on as they always have; I see people and institutions making plans for tomorrow as if it will be a replica of yesterday. Where I do see energy for facing difficulties, I find little sense of urgency. I get the sense that people hope it will all go away if we just keep our heads down and keep putting one foot ahead of the other.[6]

One goal of this book is to provide an early measuring stick that can assist congregations in evaluating their own movement into this new period of church life. I maintain that not everything of the past is ineffective and best discarded; nor will everything we try in the future be successful. We do need to address the new realities around us by the way we define "church," how we engage in evangelism, and by our discovery of the most effective strategies for mission. Evaluation of our progress involves looking at the whole ministry of the people of God as well as that of the professional staff. Chapter 4 will examine this process more fully. We must first, however, look more closely at what it means to be a church in this early stage of the postmodern era.

One Nation Under God?

The mission field has moved. It is no longer "over there," as it was in the Christendom era. Our time is more like the apostolic age in that the mission field is right in front of us. Approximately 50 percent of any community in the United States is basically unchurched, slightly more in urban areas and slightly less in rural areas and small towns.[7] Barna Institute research reports that even though the nation's population is increasing and people are exhibiting a real interest in things "spiritual," congregations suffered a net loss of membership during the 1990s. The average weekly attendance went from 99 adults in 1990 to 90 in 2000.[8] Alan Klaas conducted a two-year study for the three largest Lutheran church bodies to explore reasons for such declining membership. His two major findings: the most potent contributor to decline is the change from a churched to an unchurched society in America, and the best hope for addressing these changes lies within the individual congregation.[9]

Growing up in the '40s, '50s and even '60s, children in many communities started the morning with prayer in public school. Religious holidays were observed as unofficial national ones. Nativity scenes were found on courthouse squares. Vestiges of this era could still be found when I moved to Dallas, Texas, in 1976. When I presented an out-of-state driver's license with a local check, a friendly store clerk asked me, "Are you new in town? How do you like it here? Have you found a church home yet?" In my first parish the regular attenders were defined as those who came every Sunday. These were the decades when no one considered leaving the space for church affiliation blank on a hospital admittance form. Everyone had some background upon which to draw. Casual inquiry as to where one went to church was commonplace. The major faith groups were Protestant, Catholic, and Jewish.

Generation X, born between 1965 and 1980, is the first generation that, en masse, was not taken to church. Their baby-boomer parents turned against organized religion and left the church in droves. I jointly officiated at a recent wedding where the only Christian scripture the young couple could remember was 1 Corinthians 13, the famous passage on love. After the service a 20-something woman approached me and said, "That was a lovely poem you read. Where could I get a copy of it?" This is a generation of adults, now raising families of their own, who know the words to only the secular holiday songs and stumble over the verses of "Away in a Manger." Even the definition of "regular attender" has changed. People who attend worship once a month consider themselves "active." The very expression "church home" has shifted as well. Alan Klaas, in research for his book *In Search of the Unchurched*, discovered that in an unchurched society people might report that they attended XYZ congregation. What they meant was that they attended once or twice a year, or perhaps less.[10] Barna's research is even more interesting in its discovery that one in six adults surveyed selects a group of churches—anywhere from two to five—and attends each of them sporadically rather than choosing just one.[11] A secular culture is no longer friendly to religion in the public school, civic arena, or workplace. Employees can lose their jobs if they are perceived to be pushing their personal religious beliefs. Yet contradictions are typical of postmodernism. During the tragedy of September 11, 2001, and after the loss of the space shuttle Columbia in February 2003, public officials used highly religious language, referred to "God," and implied a belief in "heaven" in their public statements. One determined Indiana Christian responded to a law decreeing "no nativity scene on public property" by placing one in the back of his pick-up truck and parking it in front of the county courthouse each day of the holiday season. Despite public controversy, he was ruled to be acting within his civil rights, so long as he kept the parking meter fed.

It isn't easy for pastors and other church leaders to understand or respond to postmodernism. It forces us to examine both what we do and how we do it. It strikes to the very core of our being and requires that, once again, we open ourselves to God's transformation. If we are not willing to do so, we risk becoming isolated from the culture in which we live, inviting stagnation and further decline. The question before us is, Will the church in the postmodern world become a museum or a movement? Will we become, like the apostolic church, a missional community, or will we remain inwardly focused, continuing to do the same things and working harder at it, but hoping for a different outcome? I share the feeling of others that if Christianity is to be faithful to the gospel calling, or even to survive, we Christians must reinvent ourselves. Truth, whether sacred or secular, is always expressed in culturally rooted symbols. We must learn to communicate the truth of Jesus Christ in ways that speak to the postmodern culture in which God has placed us.

The Task Ahead

Between 70 percent and 85 percent of unchurched people state that spirituality is important or very important to their lives. One recent survey revealed that between 40 percent and 60 percent of unchurched people reported that they pray to God daily or weekly. These are neighbors, co-workers and teens who sit next to you at a ballgame, people who describe themselves as "spiritual" but "not religious." Most people who grew up in the church of Christendom have great difficulty understanding this distinction. Why would anyone who believes in God not want to go to church? This, however, appears to be true for more than 70 million people living in the United States.[12] Postmodern Americans have separated the miracle of faith from the act of participating in the life of a congregation.

The encouraging news is that the postmodern culture does offer many new opportunities to witness to the gospel. Community is in short supply in contemporary life. More and more people are finding our world a frightening place in which to live and are looking for a safe haven. Individuals and families are seeking support for such problems as dealing with divorce, drugs and alcohol, or child rearing. Most important is that people are longing for hope.[13] The recognition of the essentially spiritual nature of life; the longing for community; the burning desire for authenticity in leaders and in all relationships; and the recognition of truth in paradox, images, and story are only a few of the opportunities upon which we can build our future ministries.[14]

In the literature of "practice," those books and resources focusing primarily on the "how-tos" of ministry, you will find endless prescriptions for what needs to be done in our effort to transform the institutional church and to reach the unchurched. Many of these are referenced in this book. (I would also recommend to the reader the Congregational Resource Guide, a cooperative venture of the Indianapolis Center for Congregations, a program of the Lilly Endowment, and the Alban Institute, which has the most complete and up-to-date listing and description of resources for congregations. This list is available online at http://www.congregationalresources.org.)

Paul Wilkes, a writer and television producer, set out to discover what makes a congregation excellent. Through the generosity of the Lilly Endowment, Wilkes and his research team studied hundreds of parishes looking for what the writer Flannery O'Connor called "a habit of being," congregations with a soul.[15] Looking for congregations that were growing and thriving, the Parish/Congregation Study, conducted through the University of North Carolina, sought to learn what was working and how success could be reproduced in congregations of a variety of sizes. In 2001 the findings were published in two books, *Excellent Catholic Parishes: The Guide to Best Places and Practices*[16], and *The Best Protestant Congregations: The Guide to Best Places and Practices*. The criteria used when selecting parishes and congregations included these:

- A joyful spirit is evident.
- The community is welcoming and accessible to everyone.
- Worship is innovative, thoughtful, alive, and relevant.
- A significant bond exists between members, and true community exists.
- Teaching and preaching are scripture based.
- The church reaches out to people and needs in the immediate area and beyond.
- Leadership is conscious of the diversity of members, and able to adapt.
- The ministry emphasizes deep relationship with God and true spirituality.

- Decisions are made collaboratively, involving broad lay leadership.
- Worship honors Christian tradition but is not static.
- Leadership boldly confronts real problems within membership and community.
- The church is not content with its successes.[17]

Some of the congregations reflect the very best of the modern-era church; others reflect the best of the first wave of postmodern churches. Most of them reflect the transition we're in—sorting through what continues to build up Christ's church while constantly looking for ways to be fully relevant in today's culture. Brian McLaren, an author and the pastor of Cedar Ridge Community Church, an innovative congregation in Spencerville, Maryland (between Baltimore and Washington, D.C.) calls this becoming "the church on the other side." My observations of the world and the response of most churches lead me to agree with this statement of McLaren's: "The degree of change we are experiencing now is such that small measures, even a lot of them, aren't enough. Instead, we need major change, qualitative change, revolution, rebirth, reinvention, and not just once, but repeatedly for the foreseeable future."[18] A renewed congregation is good, but a reinvented congregation is better. Reinvention means true transformation, not just redevelopment.

The Reinvented Church

What will be the character of the reinvented church? Only God knows! It will most likely include multiple models and definitions. The Barna Institute suggests several scenarios for postmodern Christianity. One expression might be a return to the house church, with small groups of Christians meeting in homes for worship, study, and sharing, thus addressing the desire for intimacy and simplicity in today's culture. Another expression of the faith community could be a "cyberchurch." Barna predicts that between 10 percent and 20 percent of the population will use the Internet to address their spiritual needs by the year 2010.[19] Such a community might approximate the new-paradigm churches modeled after the Vineyard churches or Calvary chapels studied by Donald Miller. Successful churches in the postmodern world might resemble Ginghamsburg United Methodist Church in Tipp City, Ohio, or Prince of Peace Lutheran Church in suburban Minneapolis—both churches of mainline denominations that have radically reshaped their ministries to reach out to a postmodern world.

Loren Mead's challenges to the emerging church of the 21st century provide a helpful starting point for reinventing the church. Mead says he believes that the cornerstones of faithfulness will include transferring the "ownership" of the church from the clergy back to the laity, designing or revamping our organizational structures, discovering a passionate spirituality, feeding the world's need for community, and becoming an apostolic people.[20] Each of these characteristics is consistent with postmodern thinking. To plan our ministries to fulfill these needs adequately requires evaluation, redesign, and considerable letting go of much that has been important to us in the past.

Reinvention requires change. Sometimes the change includes a return to what we once did well. In other instances it means stepping into uncharted waters. Whether we're developing totally new models or radically revamping existing ones, change is the constant.

A Price to Pay

Everything has a cost. We know this in our heart, and yet we try to avoid it. We want the "old" church just as it was, with comforting hymns, informally claimed pews, and familiar liturgies. We also want the benefits of the "new church," full of young families and hope for the future. We want new believers who mature in Christ and share the responsibilities of church membership. We don't want anyone mad—ever! We want it both ways. We want the comfort of the past and the promise of the future without alienating anyone.

Mike Regele was among the first to suggest that becoming a postmodern church would have a price tag. To become "the church on the other side" we will have to give up customs and practices that have nurtured us and some that we hold dear. It's more than just the changes in congregational life and programming that we know must come; it's a change of mind-set, which becomes the transition point from what has been to what could be. In the 21st century we'll need to let go of the expectation that the church has a favored position in the mainstream of culture. We cannot assume that an unchurched culture will continue to provide financial and legal exemptions for religious organizations. We may become more like some other institutions—taxed. Seminaries must relinquish the belief that they can adequately prepare students for ministry and face the reality that today a theological education that relies primarily on Bible and theology fulfills only one part of preparing pastors for service. The cultural and racial-ethnic diversity that is normative in postmodern life will demand that congregations acquire new skills in relating to those around them. It is in the laboratory of everyday life that we will learn to become a multicultural church. Denominations will need to renegotiate their relationship to local congregations. We must see the congregation as the front line of Christianity and the most important vehicle for mission. Christians need to acknowledge the presence of other major religious worldviews. We are required to present the Christian story as the authoritative witness to God's love of humanity while recognizing and, I daresay, respecting the fact that it is one of many stories being told today.[21]

Congregations will be challenged to give up such cherished beliefs as these:

- If we build it, they will come.
- New members will join because of the pastor.
- If we can reach the children, they'll bring their parents.
- The pastor is the leader of the congregation.
- Adding a worship service will destroy our feeling of "oneness."

- The church exists primarily to meet the needs of those within it, rather than those who do not yet know Christ.

The list goes on and on. Most readers already suspect that these beliefs no longer hold true. The big question is, Are we willing to pay the price for reinvention? Brian McLaren points out that "[t]he world of religion has a fine way of baptizing the last era and riding it until the next era is nearly over."[22] We can try to wait it out, trusting in practices that no longer work but needing more "proof" that the new way can be better. Or, as Alan Roxburgh suggests, we can "help form genuine communities that are shaped by the distinctive practices of Christian identity"[23] and pray that God will bless our efforts. I hope that we'll choose the latter. Either way we choose, things will never be the same.

POSTMODERN EVALUATION: THE DILEMMA

3

WE ALL WANT OUR CHURCH TO BE SUCCESSFUL. WE ALL WANT our pastor to succeed. Why then, is it so difficult for churches to conduct meaningful, regular evaluations? I addressed this and other issues of evaluation in my earlier book *Evaluating Ministry: Principles and Processes for Clergy and Congregations.*[1] Let it suffice to say that most congregations are in a quandary about the whats, whens, and hows of evaluation. Evaluations are often used in negative, unhelpful ways to resolve pastoral difficulties and to justify the termination of relationships. "Annual performance reviews" can be routine, sterile, and relatively unproductive for both the pastor or staff member and for the review committee conducting the process (called the personnel committee in some denominations). It's no wonder pastors are wary about review times. Even in the most positive circumstances, evaluating pastors and staff is often separated from evaluating the effectiveness in ministry of the congregation as a whole. Since the pastor and members are in partnership to conduct the mission of the congregation, reviewing only one partner often leads to an incomplete picture. In addition to evaluating the pastor's effectiveness, the process presented in this book provides opportunity to reflect on the congregation's effectiveness in each area. I hope this methodology will highlight the unique contribution that both pastor and congregation make to the overall success of the church.

Unless a review results in meaningful conversation, changed behavior, or more effective ministry, it isn't a good use of anyone's time. Why are ministry reviews not more worthwhile? I believe that in many cases it's because *what* we're evaluating and *how* we're evaluating is still tied to a modern-era understanding of successful ministry.

Evaluation is elusive because it is both objective and subjective. The modern world ignored this tension by trying to make everything measurable, believing that if something couldn't be quantified, it couldn't be evaluated. Some important aspects of ministry can be measured, but other things, equally important, cannot. What I regard as great preaching may seem mediocre to you. I may describe my pastor as "warm," and you may experience her as "aloof." Most modern-era congregations ignored the subjective and chose to measure only a few basic statistics such as worship attendance or the results of stewardship efforts.[2] Some congregations would review their pastor's performance on the basis of a series of goals that could be quantitatively evaluated. Adherence to management by objectives, the establishment of measurable goals, and the importance of time lines have been vitally important to the modern-era church. It was believed that these tools for review assured fair, objective evaluation and provided what the rational modernist could trust—hard data. Many readers know, however, that there has always been much more to measuring effective ministry than how many people joined the church in the past year. On the hearts of most reviewers was the lingering question: What role should the subjective side of ministry play in any staff member's evaluation? Furthermore, whose subjective opinion should count when evaluation time rolls around—the review team's? the formal board's? the largest financial contributor's? Most modern congregations found it easier to take the "Joe Friday" approach. When confronted with an emotional witness, the lead detective in the old "Dragnet" television series would always play it safe by saying, "Just the facts, ma'am." As important as facts are, the postmodern world is open to other sources of information.

The Dimensions of Evaluation

The goal of an evaluation or review process should always be to improve the ministry of a congregation and the effectiveness of its members and staff. The challenge for today's church is finding the balance in all dimensions of effective evaluation. Improving ministry means considering data that are partly technical (objective) and partly value-based (opinion).[3] Engaging both sources of information can lead to productive change. Jeff Woods, in his excellent book *User-Friendly Evaluation: Improving the Work of Pastors, Programs, and Laity*, identifies two aspects of evaluation. *Summative* evaluation looks at the concrete, factual basis of whether the person is fulfilling the position description, completing the tasks assigned, and so forth. The second is what Woods calls *formative* evaluation, which focuses on the improvement of the person's performance in the position. The subjective dimension of evaluation enters here. An employee may fulfill a basic requirement of a position but do so with little or no energy or creativity. The pastor may lead a weekly Bible study, but her teaching methods may leave much to be desired. Woods suggests that 90 percent of any evaluation should be formative.[4] Assisting staff members to fulfill their responsibilities and to move toward excellence is equally important.

Besides these two aspects of professional review, I would add a third dimension—that time-honored practice of discernment; that is, the process of listening to God and then developing a "vision" for where the church might go. The act of confirming and refining the vision with others in the congregation and then executing it is what we call "leadership." How does the pastor understand God's leading in his or her ministry? What does the pastor believe God is calling this church to do? How is the pastor shaping his or her understanding of God's intended direction in conversation with other leaders in the congregation? This dimension of evaluation falls into the subjective range.

Whether a pastor or staff member effectively exercises such discernment as a leader is often measured by whether the outcomes of leadership are personally pleasing to the evaluators. If they believe the church is moving in a positive direction, they are more likely to affirm the pastor's discernment. If, however, they disagree with the direction the church is taking, they may not judge the pastor's vision so positively. This aspect of a review may initially be awkward. The church is unaccustomed to talking about the pastor's discernment process. It is, however, an important conversation to begin. God's vision for ministry in a particular place does not belong solely to the pastor or solely to the members. Reflecting together on how each listens for God can deepen a sense of partnership and add new richness to the dialogue.

The Question of Leadership

Whether the approach is summative ("How well did our pastor provide leadership to the church board this last year?") or formative ("How can our pastor be more effective in leading us through change?"), the question of what constitutes good leadership creeps into all reviews. We expect our pastor to be our leader. We look to members of the staff to lead us in various aspects of our mission. Leadership is one of the most-discussed topics in contemporary society. This is also true in the world of the church. Among the many functions that make up the larger role of "pastor" is that of congregational leader. But definitions of "pastor as leader" are as numerous as the members of the church. For some, the role of leader may be "the person who equips us to do ministry." For others, the leader is "the person visible to the community who does ministry on our behalf." It is important to discuss all aspects of leadership involved in being a pastor.

Leadership can be hard to evaluate. Nicholas Imparato and Oren Harari, professors at the McLaren School of Business in San Francisco, say they believe that

The missing variable in the equation [addressing issues of performance] is an accuracy of role perception. Increasingly, the failure to boost or change performance is due neither to a lack of motivation nor to ability but rather to an inaccurate reading of the roles that need to be enacted to confront today's realities.[5]

These authors proceed to emphasize that successful leaders for the coming era will not be just like those who succeeded in previous times. New occasions call for new duties. As pastors engage in new roles, they will also need to relinquish roles that have been meaningful and productive in the past. The image of the pastor as someone who regularly visits in the home is a good example of this change. Although many postmodern families do not want or need a periodic home visit from their pastor, visitation still shows up on many evaluation forms. This custom was an important part of a pastor's weekly responsibility in the church of the '40s and '50s. Home visitation is still important to the culture of some communities, but many postmodern families expect the pastor to pay a visit only at a time of family crisis or particular need. Successful leadership in today's church is still being measured against criteria for success in a very different era of the church's existence.

Church members frequently talk about "leadership," but they often mean management. Management maintains the status quo with hopes for reasonable strength and growth in the organization. Leadership requires vision, risk taking, and change in the organization's life. Change can leave parishioners feeling unsettled or at loose ends. A term currently in vogue in church circles is "transformational." Many authors believe that the church needs to be "transformed" if it is going to carry out its mission in a postmodern world. Most people realize that transformation entails change. After all, you can't transform something without changing it. However, a little change often goes a long way in congregations. When churches say they desire a transformational leader, they usually have no idea what they're really asking for. Often they mean someone who will bring just enough change to keep the pews and the offering plates full. Pastors have historically been rewarded for being effective managers, for keeping the church stable and moving. Pastors who are transformational leaders often find that they are not universally valued or praised. When a pastor accepts a call to become a transformational leader and discovers the church wants only a small degree of change, problems arise quickly. Even under the most positive of circumstances, transformation is hard work, and the changes are often uncomfortable. Members of the review committee may find that their own level of comfort with the process of transformation affects their evaluation of the pastor who is leading the change. It is important to have open and honest discussion of these issues as part of the review process.

Robert Quinn, a professor of organizational behavior and human resource management at the Graduate School of Business, University of Michigan, Ann Arbor, talks about management and leadership in a new way in his excellent book *Deep Change*. Quinn views management as a dimension of leadership and divides the task of leading into what he calls "transactional behavior," managing the status quo well and providing stability to an organization, and "transformational behavior," which includes the more visionary and change-oriented aspects of leadership. Quinn and his colleague Stuart Hart, who conducted a study of more than 900 chief executive officers, discovered four roles that leaders play: vision setter, motivator, analyzer, and taskmaster.[6] Effective leaders move back and forth among these roles, responding to the needs of a particular moment in organizational life.

When a pastoral leader is working out of the transaction category (management), he or she is either an analyzer seeing to the efficiency of the church, constantly evaluating and dealing with conflicting needs, or a taskmaster attending to the completion of tasks, evaluating results, and solving problems. These acts are often easily measured in a summative evaluation process. Did the pastor complete the sermon series on "The Footsteps of Paul"? Did the pastor assist the vestry in resolving the day-school problem? When the pastoral leader is working out of the transformational category (vision), he or she is functioning as a motivator who instills commitment, reflecting the core values of the congregation, challenging and inspiring people to new levels of excitement and service. The pastor may serve as a vision setter who focuses on the future, keeps abreast of emerging trends, and communicates a sense of where God may next be calling the church.[7] These functions fall more into the formative arena of evaluation and emerge from the discernment of the pastor and congregational leadership.

One of the more fascinating outcomes of Quinn and Hart's research is the finding that most leaders are more drawn to the transactional roles, which can be measured and, because they're often related to the status quo, more frequently rewarded. The most successful of these skilled business executives, however, were the ones who performed out of both the transactional and transformation categories, comfortably moving among the roles of taskmaster, vision setter, analyzer, and motivator.[8] The highly successful pastors and congregations that will be used as illustrations in this book reflect the importance of moving comfortably among all four roles. They know when to maintain and when to change.

Evaluating effective leadership for the 21st-century church is an evolving process. We've depended on objective criteria for so long that it will surely be a challenge to review the more subjective categories of leadership. We will still need accountability for the management aspects of ministry, many of which can be measured. We all have a job to accomplish. The postmodern church, however, needs also to include in its reviews assessments of the more subjective dimensions, such as developing vision and demonstrating leadership. If we believe that the goal of evaluation is helping to improve ministry for all involved, then that view will likely require a new approach to evaluation, one that includes conversation about leadership and what it means for both the pastor being reviewed and the congregation.

Shift in Thinking

Most pastors who attended seminary and were ordained before 1990 were thoroughly trained to serve a modern-era church. Ministers attending seminary since that time have been in a transition period. The majority of their training has remained rooted in the modern world;

but an occasional class, usually one related to worship, has tiptoed into the postmodern. The real training ground for both groups of clergy—the parish—has reinforced most pastors' sense that members want their church to remain pretty much what it always was—a tranquil place of spiritual comfort. Clergy have been trained and rewarded for maintenance, not creativity. Preaching has been viewed as a form of teaching, not as a tool for transformation. The emphasis has been on ministering to large groups, not on developing small groups. Members have been assimilated, not transformed. The culture has been understood as the enemy, with the church standing against it. The buck has stopped with the pastors, not with congregational leadership. Church professionals have been gatekeepers, not permission givers. The mysterious has been viewed as irrational and thus avoided. A growing number of pastors, however, are learning what it might take to lead congregations into this new era. I spend many hours with pastors who feel caught between the new postmodern possibilities that they encounter in workshops and books, and the anxiety their parishioners feel about even the smallest change.[9] These pastors are frustrated that they cannot bring about church growth or the spiritual renewal for which they long because of the deep emotional ties their parishioners have to the past. Many pastors feel that they are tapping with one foot and waltzing with the other as they dance gingerly through the minefields of this transitional period. Even forward-thinking clergy sometimes believe that when annual review time rolls around, it's safer (and saner) to talk about their plans for the tried-and-true—preaching, teaching, and pastoral care. They prefer sticking to safe topics than venturing into the anxiety-producing waters of change.

The amount of time and energy that goes into a performance review should result in a plan that strengthens the ministry for both the staff member under review and the congregation. Too often no such plan emerges. Most evaluation reports result in little change.[10] Could that be because the evaluation process itself is limited to that which can be measured, when the growing edge for a particular pastor lies in other, less measurable areas? What would happen if congregations adopted a new approach to evaluation, one that considers objective data, subjective reflection, and group discernment based on emerging postmodern criteria?

A New Model

Thomas Harvey, professor of business at La Verne University in La Verne, California, declares that "Good management is less a science than an art form."[11] I would say that good *evaluation* also is less a science than an art form. Note that I didn't suggest that no science is involved. There is, indeed, a place for measurement. Many good models are available for conducting such an evaluation. What I offer in the following chapters is a process that

- is more formative than summative,
- is based on both personal reflection and deep dialogue,
- involves interested stakeholders and formal decision makers,
- emphasizes mutual ministry of both church professionals and church members, and
- introduces postmodern criteria for effectiveness.

In an earlier book I identified three outcomes of evaluation that pastors and review teams could anticipate—the emergence of new realizations, the setting of new goals and directions, and the exploration of the mysterious relationship between pastor and members.[12] Those still stand. The model I propose here will invite the reviewers into these outcomes from a new vantage point, that of mutual learners.

This review model starts with 12 characteristics of an effective 21st-century pastor. I have developed these characteristics through my research, personal observation, and interviews with clergy who are widely acknowledged to be effective in leading the modern-era church into a postmodern ministry. These characteristics will be described in more detail in the following chapters:

1. The ability to maintain personal, professional, and spiritual balance.
2. The ability to guide a transformational faith experience (conversion).
3. The ability to motivate and develop a congregation to be a "mission outpost" (help churches reclaim their role in reaching new believers).
4. The ability to develop and communicate a vision.
5. The ability to interpret and lead change.
6. The ability to promote and lead spiritual formation for church members.
7. The ability to provide leadership for high-quality, relevant worship experiences.
8. The ability to identify, develop, and support lay leaders.
9. The ability to build, inspire, and lead a "team" of both staff and volunteers.
10. The ability to manage conflict.
11. The ability to navigate successfully the world of technology.
12. The ability to be a lifelong learner.

The model in this book, "Reflecting on Ministry," contains an instrument to be completed by the pastor and one to be completed by the review committee. Both are based on the 12 characteristics of an effective 21st-century pastor. Reflecting my strong belief that effective evaluation of a pastor or staff member also includes evaluation of the congregation's ministry, both instruments contain questions about the church's effectiveness in various areas. Of course, it is difficult to conduct a helpful review unless the members are familiar with how the pastor or the congregation is fulfilling ministry responsibilities. Members of the review committee who feel they don't have the firsthand knowledge to judge the effectiveness of the church or the pastor in a particular area will find this an opportunity to inquire of those who do know. Variations of this process for the review of associate pastors and volunteer staff are included in appendixes C, D, and E.

For those readers who would like to make changes to the instruments for use within their congregations, a Microsoft Word version of "Reflecting on Ministry" is available for download from the Alban Institute's Web site, at http://www.alban.org/BookDetails.asp?ID=1809. The resource is free for those who have purchased this book. Readers will need the book with them to access the instrument.

STEP 1

Personal Reflection. The first step in the review/evaluation process is the pastor's self-evaluation. Appendix A is a reflection instrument titled "A Pastor's Personal Evaluation." It includes numerous reflection questions on each of the 12 characteristics. Because the instrument is comprehensive, the pastor may wish to complete it in several sittings, or time blocks. An alternative would be for the pastor to take a solitary retreat and slowly to work his or her way through the questions, returning to them between times of study and prayer. The key is to approach the reflection fresh and rested. Each area deserves the pastor's best thoughts and plans. It is important not to rush these reflections, as they combine both the summative and formative aspect of review. Discernment is demonstrated as the pastor prepares action steps related to each characteristic. The compilation of these steps becomes the initial "action plan" for the pastor's future ministry, which will be refined in consultation with an invited group and finally with the review committee. It is recommended that the congregation's official board see this plan. If major changes in the pastor's responsibility or goals are identified in the action plan, these should be shared with the congregation.

STEP 2

Feedback Group. Generally, members of the congregation officially selected to manage the church's personnel policies conduct annual reviews. Most formal evaluations do not include the participation of individuals whom the pastor has chosen. In *Checklist for Change,* Thomas Harvey says, "To turn evaluation into the first stage of change, choose a team of interested insiders. Lead team members to view themselves not merely as evaluators but as change agents. Forming a combined evaluation and change team leads to better, more usable, data."[13] Allowing the pastor to invite some people with whom he or she is comfortable to begin the review process and perhaps collaborate on the initial action plan lowers anxiety and often helps the pastor hear constructive feedback in a more positive way.[14] Dialogue contributes to a formative evaluation. A pastoral evaluation should not be *done to* the pastor but rather *done with* the pastor.[15]

The dialogue begins with the feedback group after the pastor has completed the "reflecting on ministry" form. I recommend that the pastor invite no more than three to five members of the church to participate in this process. Each of these members will receive a copy of the completed reflection instrument, including the action plan, before the feedback meeting so that they may prepare for the conversation. A minimum of two hours should be set aside for the dialogue between the pastor and these members. During this time the group can discuss with the pastor any discrepancies between the self-evaluation rating and how the group experiences the pastor. Each step in the pastor's action plan should also be discussed. Using the feedback received in this meeting, the pastor may revise his or her reflections or action plan before providing it to the review committee at least one week before the review. The comments of the feedback group are shared with the personnel committee only as they are incorporated in the revised action plan. The review committee receives only the pastor's personal evaluation and the revised action plan.

STEP 3

The Review Committee. While the pastor is completing the process described above, the review committee will be completing the instrument found in Appendix B, "Reflecting on Ministry: The Review Committee Evaluation." This form provides a numerical scale by which to assess the church's and pastor's effectiveness in each of the 12 characteristics. Space should be provided for comments after each question. Each member should be given several weeks to complete the forms to provide time for research, if needed. The completed forms are given to the chairperson of the committee or to that person's designee for compilation.

The evaluation numbers are listed for each area on the compiled form, and the comments are listed under each characteristic being reviewed. The final, compiled version is provided to all members of the committee and to the pastor at least one week before the formal review.

The Review. The pastor and the review committee should schedule a minimum of 90 minutes for the review conversation. A longer time may be needed the first year the process is used. For first use of this model, one option is to conduct the review in two separate meetings. The time needed to conduct the review in subsequent years would likely be less. It is helpful to begin the review on a positive note—what can be celebrated? The review should include conversation about the pastor's evaluation, the review committee's evaluation, and any discrepancies between them. Are there areas for growth seen by the review committee that the pastor has not acknowledged? Did the pastor rate congregational effectiveness lower than the review committee did on some of the characteristics? Are there any surprises in the documents?

The second part of the review should include consideration of the pastor's action plan for the next year. Although the action plan is the pastor's own plan for ministry, it should be developed in the context of the larger vision of the congregation, which the pastor developed with other congregational leaders. Further refinement of the action plan can be based on the insights of the review, including whether it is consistent with the congregation's mission.

Both the review committee chairperson and the pastor should formally sign the summary of the review, including the action plan and any additional comments or agreements. A copy of the signed document will be given to the pastor and a copy placed in the pastor's personnel file.

FUTURE REVIEWS

The initial completion of "Reflecting on Ministry" is comprehensive. This occasion may be the first time the pastor and review committee have discussed some of the issues raised. Churches that adopt this process will find that subsequent reviews require much less work. The pastor and review committee should feel free to revise any of the steps in this review process to meet the pastor's and congregation's needs, once the original model has been put into operation. The model can be used in its entirety on an annual basis or easily adapted. Some review committees may wish to conduct the entire process every three years with annual "updates" and evaluation of the action plan in the intervening years. Some pastors may choose to invite a feedback group in alternate years. Each year the pastor's action plan should be reviewed. What has been completed? What was not accomplished and why? What is in progress? What is no longer relevant? The key to using the model is to stay focused on the 12 characteristics.

To make best use of the model, the review team must become familiar with the rationale for these characteristics. Chapter 4 will prepare the pastor; the feedback group, and the review committee to understand better the meaning and importance of these characteristics to vital 21st-century ministry.

THE HEART OF THE MATTER: 12 CHARACTERISTICS FOR EFFECTIVE 21ST-CENTURY MINISTRY

ONE AFTERNOON WHILE I WAS RIFLING THROUGH BACKED-UP periodicals, the tag line for an advertisement caught my attention: "Think Differently about Ministry in Order to Minister Differently!" The ad showed three pastors. Two, photographed in black and white, were dressed in traditional clergy attire. The third, positioned between these two, wearing casual clothes and sunglasses, leaped off the page in living color. The ad's subhead asked, "Ready to do something different?"

The ad was promoting a doctor of ministry degree program, claiming that this particular seminary could point the degree seeker in a new direction. Most of us know that it takes more than forsaking clerical collars to be effective in ministry today. It requires an ongoing consideration of what should remain at the bedrock of ministry and where change should occur. It requires that both pastor and congregation truly struggle to discern what's working and what's not, what needs to be added, and what has to be retired to make room for God's new vision of ministry.

Martin Copenhaver, senior pastor of the Wellesley Congregational Church in Wellesley, Massachusetts, calls pastors "the last generalists" in a world of increasing specialization. Copenhaver says, "A pastor's work is not simply distinct tasks performed at different times. Rather, the various tasks relate to each other in dynamic ways, setting each one into a richer context."[1] He calls for a revival of pastoral imagination to help pastors, once again, fall in love with their vocation. Gil Rendle, senior consultant at the Alban Institute, also believes that congregations can best be served by those whom he calls "deep" generalists. In his excellent article "The Leadership We Need—Negotiating Up, Not Down," Rendle says this about leadership for the future: "We would need to move outside of cultural norms to value the strange gifts our new leaders would bring. Those leaders would need to be exceptionally mature and able to stand outside of cultural norms, knowing that their gifts are valuable."[2] I agree with both authors that the vast majority of 21st-century pastors will need to be generalists. The fast-paced, constantly changing world in which we find ourselves demands diverse skills. Pastors who want to specialize may simply be out of date by the time they finish their training. I believe that effective pastors will be those whose ministries are rooted in the general but critical characteristics listed in the previous chapter. This chapter introduces and explores more completely each of these characteristics. At the end of each description, I have included the questions for the characteristic that the pastor and the review committee will consider in the "Reflecting on Ministry" instruments. These are compiled and presented as instruments in appendices A and B.

Characteristic 1: The Ability to Maintain
Personal, Professional, and Spiritual Balance

In a study of 925 pastors in the Presbyterian Church (U.S.A.), 75 percent of the responders said that finding time for recreation, relaxation, or personal reflection was a "great problem" or "somewhat of a problem." Fifty-two percent of the same group said that having a private life apart from their ministerial role was very difficult.[3] Concern for the pastor's emotional and spiritual health rises when we consider that most Sundays the pastor is the worship *leader* and only occasionally gets to worship with his or her family. The rate of clergy burnout appears to be at an all-time high. In my own practice of ministry I speak regularly with pastors from both within my judicatory and across the wider faith community. Depression and fatigue are frequent concerns shared with me. The stress of constantly ministering to those in need, often in the most difficult moments of life, can mount up over time. Even the welcome demands of Christmas, Lent, and Easter add 36 additional points on one clergy stress scale![4] Many denominational health plans are facing hefty financial challenges in covering the medical expenses for the stress-related illnesses of clergy. Marriages and family life suffer from inadequate attention, and clergy divorce is all too common. Moreover, pastors often graduate from seminary with a huge financial debt, only to receive a starting salary barely above that of a new college graduate beginning an entry-level position in a different field. Financial worries are among the top concerns for clergy families.

Ronald Heifetz and Marty Linsky, faculty members of the John F. Kennedy School of Management at Harvard University, raise important questions for us in their wonderful book *Leadership on the Line—Staying Alive through the Dangers of Leading*: "Who's holding the holder? When you are completely exhausted from being the containing vessel, who will provide you with a place to meet your need for intimacy and release?"[5] If these authors raise questions about secular leaders, how much more critical are these issues for pastors and members of church staffs who, day in and day out, care for the emotional and spiritual needs of the people they serve? When an exhausted pastor who has not engaged in self-care faces an annual review, the stakes seem high to that pastor. Any feedback can strike the pastor as criticism and all comments as personal. Tired pastors cannot separate themselves from their role performance, and even a constructive critique may feel like a personal attack. Ministry in the postmodern world is hard, and a pastor must keep emotionally and spiritually fit. It is even more important for 21st-century pastors to engage in self-care. Protecting and honoring days off, keeping a personal sabbath (usually *not* a Sunday), and always taking the full number of vacation days allowed are some of the ways effective pastors care for themselves.

The demands of ministry can produce tension in clergy families. "I think the most significant influence on my pastoral life has been my family. Early on I determined that I was never going to treat my parishioners better than I treated my family."[6] This comment from author and retired pastor Eugene Peterson points to a central issue for most clergy. Both single and married clergy need to spend time with their families and non-church-related friends. Both groups have loved ones and relationships that require time for nurture and renewal—just like anyone else. Family and other important relationships provide the emotional context that encourages a minister to put down the role of pastor and put on the role of spouse, parent, son or daughter, sibling, or friend. Mike Foss, senior pastor of Prince of Peace Lutheran Church in Burnsville, Minnesota, a truly "postmodern" congregation, notes: "The more successful the pastor, the less approachable his or her family is and the more isolated they become. This impacts the marriage. My wife, Christine, and I search out a few people with whom we can 'be real.' This has been essential for us!"[7] Effective pastors build time with loved ones into their schedules and safeguard it.

The first and last of seven values for the leadership and staff of Willow Creek Community Church in South Barrington, Illinois, reflect a deep awareness of the importance of the personal spiritual journey for Christ's professional servants. The first value is "Lead a spiritually surrendered life"; the last is "Get on your knees."[8] The importance of the pastor's own spiritual journey cannot be overemphasized. When asked, "What goes into the making of a spiritual leader?" Alban Institute senior consultant and author Roy Oswald replied, "Who you are is more important than what you do."[9] If a pastor wishes to encourage the growth of a spiritually mature congregation, that pastor must also be on a personal spiritual journey. A well-developed prayer life, Bible study not connected to sermon preparation, periodic retreats, work with a spiritual director, and engagement in other spiritual disciplines—these are some of the ways that effective pastors meet this need. Congregations need to encourage pastors to care for their spiritual lives.

Physical health is an often-overlooked topic in a pastor's annual review. This, of course, is a very personal issue and one for which the pastor is ultimately responsible. No one would think of slapping the pastor's hand as she reaches for the chocolate cake at a covered-dish supper! Yet in a large national survey of pastors it was discovered that 66 percent of those surveyed were either overweight (46 percent) or obese (30 percent) according to the Body-Mass Index, a standard for assessing weight relative to height.[10] It is important for the review committee to ask if the pastor has a yearly physical. It is not invasive to ask if the pastor is making time for exercise. Postmodern churches might regard a pastor's annual membership in the health club as important an investment as a week's study leave. It is not the job of the church to monitor the pastor's overall health. It *is* the responsibility of the church to advocate for good health-care strategies.

In a fascinating essay titled "Ten Things I Didn't Learn in Seminary," John Esau, a retired pastor from North Newton, Kansas, says, "We pastors have to create our own support group; the church won't and can't do it for us."[11] In a seminar I lead jointly with Alban Institute senior consultant Roy Oswald each summer, we always ask, "How many of you are part of a regular support group?"[12] Over the years we have seen participation in a support group grow from only a handful to almost half the 2003 seminar participants. Successful 21st-century pastors know they cannot do it alone; they value the support and wisdom of respected colleagues. Mike Foss meets with a self-selected ecumenical support group of senior pastors of large congregations. They spend time in prayer, personal conversation, and feedback on ministry issues.[13] Ginghamsburg United Methodist Church's thoroughly postmodern pastor, Mike Slaughter, has an accountability group from the church board. He invites three members, all of whom Mike describes as "successful in their own careers," to meet with him every other Thursday. It is here that he speaks of his own struggles and successes. Much informal evaluation takes place with these people who know Mike and also know the congregation.[14] Whether a pastor chooses an accountability group from within the parish or outside it, having a place where one can share the joys, defeats, and frustrations of ministry is an invaluable tool for professional care.

Serving the church today demands so much more of a pastor than it did in an era when things were somewhat more predictable. The pastor faces a new era of ministry in which many ideas are still unproved, when the tried and true may or may not work, and when expectations for ministry come from both the modern era and from the emerging postmodern one. Maintaining personal, professional, and spiritual balance is essential to dealing with all these conflicting forces. Self-care is essential to being an effective postmodern leader.

QUESTIONS FOR THE PASTOR ON MAINTAINING PERSONAL, PROFESSIONAL, AND SPIRITUAL BALANCE

1. How often do I engage in the following?
   - Personal prayer not related to role or function of ministry
   - Bible study not related to the practice of ministry
   - A private spiritual retreat
   - The practice of faithful stewardship
2. How often do I participate in worship when I am not the leader?
3. Do I have a spiritual director or spiritual friend with whom I meet at least monthly for prayer and reflection on my own spiritual journey?
4. Do I participate in an accountability/support group other than a ministerial association?
5. How many days off do I consistently take each week?
6. Do I take all my vacation? Do I take at least one portion in a two-week block?
7. How much time is reserved for home life? (For example, four nights a week? Two nights? Saturdays?)
8. *For married pastors*: How often do I have "date" nights or other regular opportunities for special time with my spouse?

9. *For single pastors*: Do I spend time with friends or other family members on a weekly basis?
10. Do I have friends who are not members of the congregation?
11. Do I have a personal therapist or pastoral counselor identified for times of need?
12. Do I have an annual physical?
13. How often do I engage in physical exercise lasting at least 30 minutes?
14. How balanced is my current diet?
15. Am I more than 10 pounds over the recommended weight for my height?
16. Do I take a multivitamin daily?
17. Do I have interests or hobbies outside the church?

QUESTIONS FOR THE REVIEW COMMITTEE ON THE PASTOR'S MAINTENANCE OF PERSONAL, PROFESSIONAL AND SPIRITUAL BALANCE

Note: Questions for the Review Committee are to be answered using the rating scale found in appendix B.

1. How effective is our Review Committee in encouraging the overall health of our pastor?
2. How effective is our pastor in maintaining and exemplifying a balanced lifestyle?

Characteristic 2: The Ability to Guide a Transformational Faith Experience

Several years ago a pastor told me the following story. He was sitting in his suburban church office around the noon hour when he heard a gentle knock on his door. Looking up, he saw a professionally dressed woman in her late 20s. "Are you the minister here?" she asked. The pastor invited her in, and she proceeded to tell him that she had decided to explore this "religion thing," was taking her lunch hour, and had about 20 minutes to learn everything she needed to know about Christianity. My friend was floored but quickly remembered a seminary professor saying, "If you can't explain it to an eight-year-old, you shouldn't be in the business!" He briefly outlined the Christian story for her. As she was leaving, he said, "Wait! I'd like for you to take a copy of the Bible with you. This is our religious book." He turned to his bookshelf and, to his total dismay, saw nothing but his study Bibles. He scanned the selection and pulled out the one he was most willing to part with, gave it to her, and said, "This may not be the best format for you to read but if you return tomorrow I'll trade you for a better one." That afternoon he drove to a nearby religious book store, determined never again to be without Bibles he could give away. But the woman never returned.

Most mainline seminaries do not offer a course in how to lead a person to a faith commitment. Products of the modern era, seminaries, like churches, have *assumed* that the basic Christian story is known to all and that when people embrace faith, they will join a church. The postmodern world, however, is full of potential new believers who have not heard the story. Slightly more than 50 percent of any urban/metropolitan population and slightly less than 50 percent of any rural or small-town population will consist of individuals who are not active in any religious body.[15] Many of these people have no exposure to the Christian story and get their information about people of faith only from movies, TV, or novels.

Pastors who are effective in the 21st century will be those who know how to introduce a person to Jesus, not just to the church. Over 70 percent of Christian clergy participating in the "National Clergy Survey" conducted by the Pulpit and Pew Project of Duke University indicated that one of the primary problems facing pastors in today's world was the difficulty of reaching people with the gospel.[16] Of course it is not just the pastor's job to introduce people to the gospel. The task of evangelism belongs to every Christian. It is often, however, the pastor's task to walk with individuals through a conversion experience and to help them become grounded in the faith. Roy Oswald has said he believes that this is the most important skill of all in becoming an effective postmodern pastor.[17]

Leading someone through a transformational (conversion) experience involves making a personal connection. Pastors need to be available for one-on-one time with new believers. Encouraging the newcomer to form nurturing relationships with other believers in the congregation is another important task for the pastor. The effective postmodern pastor, knowing that he or she cannot complete this process alone, will have seasoned, mature Christians ready to serve as spiritual friends to the new believer. Pastors need to teach and preach the story of faith in ways that are clear and relevant to the seeker's experience. Patience is necessary in giving the individual plenty of time to make a decision about baptism or formally joining the church. Finally, the pastor must view the new believer as possibly the very best "evangelist" in the congregation and encourage the newcomer to invite family and friends into this now meaningful faith.

The church has always taught the importance of evangelism, but the modern world benefited from cultural familiarity with the Christian faith. The postmodern world provides new and exciting opportunities for pastors to think about and plan for the inclusion of new believers in their midst.

QUESTIONS FOR THE PASTOR IN GUIDING A TRANSFORMATIONAL FAITH EXPERIENCE

1. How many new believers have I nurtured into a relationship with Christ in the past year?
2. Do I have contemporary translations of the Bible on hand which I can give away as needed?
3. Do I spend time in locations where I might meet individuals without a faith background?
4. Do I have a plan for developing new believers into mature disciples?
5. How many "mentors for new believers" have I equipped this year?

6. Does our congregation have an appropriate ritual of welcome for new members and a social event to welcome them into the congregation?
7. Do I encourage people new to the faith to invite their friends and family members into the faith as well?

QUESTIONS FOR THE REVIEW COMMITTEE ON THE PASTOR'S ABILITY TO GUIDE A TRANSFORMATIONAL FAITH EXPERIENCE

1. How effective has our church been in reaching new believers this year?
2. How effective has our pastor been in leading new believers into active faith involvement?

Characteristic 3: Ability to Motivate and Develop a Congregation to be a "Mission Outpost"

What do you get when you cross a Seventh-Day Adventist with a Presbyterian? Someone who knocks on the door but doesn't know what to say!

This joke, which has floated around my denomination for years, just about sums up the challenge for most mainline denominations. We have lost our way as evangelists. This may be because late 20th-century evangelism is, as author and pastor Brian McLaren suggests, equated with pressure. He writes, "It [evangelism] means selling God as if God were vinyl siding, replacement windows, or a mortgage refinancing service. It means shoving your ideas down someone's throat, threatening him with hell if he does not capitulate to your logic or Scripture quoting."[18]

Most pastors and members of congregations are not eager to have doors slammed in their faces or friends refuse to return their phone calls. It is no wonder that evangelism didn't make it into the "top six purposes of a congregation" as reported in a study of more than 4,000 Lutheran laypeople.[19] Nine out of 10 congregations say they are evangelistic, but most spend more on their building than they do on outreach.[20] Yet never before has the mandate to "Go into all the world and proclaim the good news to the whole creation" (Mark 16:14) been so necessary as it is in the postmodern world. The vast numbers of unchurched people make the mission field impossible to ignore. Retired Episcopal bishop Claude Payne recognized the importance of regaining a sense of the local congregation as a mission outpost and transformed the Episcopal Diocese of Texas by helping pastors and congregations to embrace this concept. In this missionary model, the primary goal is "to make disciples in accordance with the Great Commandment and the Great Commission. From discipleship and the practices and commitments it brings flow all kinds of other blessings, which include the transformation of lives"[21]

What is the role of the pastor in helping a congregation make this shift in thinking? The pastor must undo the assumption held by most congregations that evangelism is best done through a committee. A committee may be helpful in providing resources or teaching people about evangelism, but evangelism is the job of every Christian.

Sally Johnson was relieved that she didn't have to teach a Bible class to be an effective evangelist. She learned this in a small group in her church, which emphasized that everyone could be an evangelist and that there were many ways to reach people. An avid dog lover, Sally had trained dogs for her friends. She decided to use her talent as a tool for outreach. She offered a free dog-training program in a local park and publicized it in the local newspaper. As the program progressed, she developed a friendship with several of the participants who went for coffee after class. Slowly Sally began to talk about her church and eventually about her faith. This story is told by Ted Haggard in his book on every-person evangelism, *Dog Training, Fly Fishing and Sharing Christ in the 21st Century*. Haggard, an evangelical pastor, workshop leader, and author, points out that "[p]eople are discipled through relationship, which is why the bulk of Scripture gives accounts of people's lives rather than a more systematic approach to Biblical principle."[22]

The effective postmodern pastor will equip the members of the congregation to see their everyday gifts as an opportunity to share the good news in ways that are comfortable and natural for them. The pastor equips members for the task of evangelism through preaching, teaching, and coaching those who feel a special gift for this ministry.

There is more to becoming a mission outpost than just bringing people to church, although the process certainly starts there. Congregations must be sensitive to the needs of those for whom being in church is a totally new experience. Later in this chapter I discuss the importance of music and worship, which speak to the heart of the potential new believer. Congregations can make visitors feel welcome in other ways. Nothing will turn off a faith explorer more than not being able to find a parking place or helpful signage to the sanctuary. Designating one or two parking places with a "Reserved for Visitors" sign signals one of two things—either that you expect only two visitors or that you *want* only two visitors. When attending Saddleback Community Church in Lake Forest, California, I was struck by the level of welcome and hospitality. This very large church had a whole parking lot reserved just for visitors. My car door was opened by a greeter, and I was directed every step of the way into the worship space. The visitor received a coupon for a free tape of the sermon, which was ready at an information booth at the end of worship.

Effective 21st-century churches realize that many visitors are "church shopping," yet these congregations have no sense of being in competition with others. They realize there are sufficient unchurched people for all congregations to grow! The message inside Saddleback's bulletin that week said something like, "We hope you'll find a home here at Saddleback, but if not, then we'll be happy to assist you in discovering another congregation that can meet your needs." The wise postmodern pastor assists new believers in discerning *which* expression of Christ's church may be the best fit for them.

Finally, it is important that the congregation have a plan for the incorporation and nurture of new believers into a deeper faith and involvement in the life of the church. Assimilation is not just the process of identifying the individual's interests and connecting them with service but also of assimilating these new members into the mature, Christian life. Ginghamsburg United Methodist Church accomplishes this by encouraging members to get involved in a cell group, through the educational program of the church, by providing opportunities to serve others in mission, and through exciting worship. Ginghamsburg Church has identified four stages of faith and involvement. They have named these cycles, each of which can last a year or more: "the curious, the convinced, the connected, and the committed."[23] Other congregations, like Zionsville Presbyterian Church, a growing congregation in an Indianapolis suburb, have designed an Academy of Discipleship offering three levels of exploration of the Christian life.[24] These congregations and many others like them recognize that becoming a disciple is more than simply joining the church.

The modern world expected the pastor to be the head evangelist. The postmodern world requires that the pastor identify and equip all members to be evangelists. The job is too big and the goal too important to trust to pastors or committees alone!

QUESTIONS FOR THE PASTOR ON MOTIVATING AND DEVELOPING THE CONGREGATION TO BE A MISSION OUTPOST

1. How many adult baptisms were performed in our congregation during the past year?
2. Is the leadership board clear about the target population this congregation is trying to reach? Is the congregation clear?
3. Do I nurture those who have a gift for evangelism through one-on-one coaching or in small-group settings?
4. Is there a formal plan for equipping members as evangelists in my congregation?
5. Have I prepared members to place the comfort of new believers above their own?
6. How many times in the past 12 months have I preached on the call to be evangelists?
7. How have we focused on being a hospitable and welcoming congregation?

8. Do we have sufficient parking spaces reserved for first-time visitors?
9. Do we have parking-lot greeters in addition to those who welcome at the church entrance?
10. To what extent is our Sunday school viewed as a tool for reaching neighborhood children and their parents?
11. Do our social-action ministries make a statement to the surrounding community that we care deeply for the poor, homeless, and marginalized people in our society?
12. Are these individuals welcomed into our church?
13. How have we collaborated with other congregations that see themselves as mission outposts in reaching the unchurched in our common community?
14. Do we have a plan for assimilating new members into the life of our congregation?

QUESTIONS FOR THE REVIEW COMMITTEE ON THE PASTOR'S ABILITY TO MOTIVATE AND DEVELOP A CONGREGATION INTO A MISSION OUTPOST

1. How effective has our church been in equipping its members to be evangelists?
2. How effective is our pastor in preaching and teaching about evangelism?
3. How effective is our pastor in supporting members who serve as evangelists?

Characteristic 4: The Ability to Develop and Communicate a Vision

Creating a meaningful vision is an exercise of both the head and the heart.[25] Most pastors have been trained by the modern church to be effective managers, but few have been freed to be visionary leaders. Yet almost every one has some quality that gently pulls them toward a larger dream for their church, a dream greater than the status quo of congregational life. Sometimes we talk about this pull as the mandate for growth, the need for change, or the call of the congregation. Robert Quinn refers to this force as the "inner voice."[26] It is here that the leader constantly works to align internal values with external realities. This effort generally leads to change and to a continuous unfolding of the vision. True vision is much more than a planning process. It is born out of a longing, a deep desire for what could be. Donald Miller's exploration of effective "new paradigm" churches noted such vision in the senior pastors leading these congregations.[27]

Bill Easum, United Methodist consultant and author, reminds us that the core vision of a Christian organization is always linked with the *ecclesia*, the belief that we are called out into the world to be disciples and to recruit followers of Jesus. Each church, however, will express that conviction in a unique way. Easum challenges congregational members to answer the question, "What is it about my experience with Jesus that this community cannot live without?"[28] The way we answer this question is the basis for our vision. Compelling vision means believing that our best days are ahead, and that God can perform remarkable acts in our midst. Brian McLaren also places the understanding of vision in a theological context. McLaren believes that vision is linked to our hope in God's ultimate promises to us. This hope, however, cannot be turned into a plan or scheme but must be more of a guiding force that permeates everything we do.[29]

The modern world defined *vision* as a strategy or plan. The postmodern world defines *vision* as an attitude, an openness, and a movement toward the possible future. The modern world approached vision as mission statements that could be printed on stationery— measurable goals and objectives and timelines. Easum posits a postmodern view that describes vision as "a song in the heart" that is "always powerful," "true to the soul," and "always apocalyptic."[30] The good news is that many congregations believe they have such a vision. The U.S. Congregational Life Survey surveyed 300,000 worshipers in over 2,000 American congregations the weekend of April 29, 2001. Seventy-one percent stated that their congregation has a clear vision for its mission and ministry.[31]

Peter Senge, Harvard Business School professor and author of the best-selling book *The Fifth Discipline*, believes that every organization has a destiny. The process of discovering this destiny is often led by the pastor, but is never solely the pastor's task. The pastor's hopes and dreams, generated by a relationship with God and with the people served, are crucial. A pastor should be able to articulate a personal vision for the congregation. However, the successful vision will always be a shared one. "At the heart of building shared vision is the task of designing and evolving ongoing processes in which people at every level of the organization, in every role, can speak from the heart about what really matters to them and be heard."[32] How effectively the pastor orchestrates this dialogue can determine whether a congregation continues to move toward God's unfolding plan or remains stuck in a predictable but less faithful place.

Twenty-first-century congregations cry out for visionary leadership. The vision comes not from the pastor, not from the people, but from God. It is the pastor's job, along with the lay leaders and other members of the church, to discover the vision God already has in mind for this congregation. So what *is* the pastor's role in uncovering this vision? I believe it is to

- set the theological and spiritual context for the vision,
- ask questions that challenge the status quo so that the vision can unfold,
- listen, listen, listen to all stakeholders, both leaders and congregants,
- serve as primary communicator and cheerleader for the vision, and
- behave as if the vision can be made real.

This is not a once-a-year process that occurs on a leadership retreat, although such an event may be helpful to anchor the vision in a time and place. The vision is not an end product but a way of life, an ongoing discovery of God's plan, which becomes real in time and place through the actions of God's people. "Visioning," then, becomes the ongoing dialogue involving God, the pastor, and the congregation. A three-year strategic plan or a five-year long-range plan is the product of the modern world. The postmodern world sees planning, visioning, and devising strategy as an ever-present part of organizational life that cannot be compartmentalized or time bound.

The structural life of the church should grow out of the vision of the congregation. Too often churches are bogged down in old committee structures that no longer serve a purpose. "Warm bodies" replace excited hearts in filling positions on boards. Staffing rationales rarely reflect the vision and mission of the congregation. The effective postmodern church will align all of its organizational life, including staff and structure, with the unfolding vision and mission of the congregation. Regular evaluation and review are essential since the vision is always in process.

Finally, the pastor lives as if he or she believes the vision is possible. It is not enough to be enthusiastic about the future. The pastor must talk, act, and lead as if the vision can and will be made real in their midst. Everything the pastor does should be anchored to this vision of the congregation.

QUESTIONS FOR THE PASTOR ON DEVELOPING AND COMMUNICATING A VISION

1. Do I annually share my personal vision for the congregation with the formal leadership board of my church? With the congregation?
2. Is our vision statement concise and easy to remember?
3. How is our vision kept before our membership (banners, letterhead, hymn, Web site, etc.)?
4. Is there a process of regular review and evaluation for the vision of the church?
5. What percentage of the congregation could articulate the vision statement?
6. How many sermons a year focus specifically on the congregation's vision?

7. Does our organizational structure equip and support the vision statement? Is it easily modified?

QUESTIONS FOR THE REVIEW COMMITTEE ON THE PASTOR'S ABILITY TO DEVELOP AND COMMUNICATE A VISION
1. How knowledgeable is our congregation about our vision?
2. How effective is our pastor in communicating the vision to our church?
3. How effective is our pastor in providing for the review and maintenance of the vision?

Characteristic 5: The Ability to Interpret and Lead Change

Do the names Sniff and Scurry or Hem and Haw mean anything to you? If so, you've probably already read physician Spencer Johnson's little book *Who Moved My Cheese?* (1998), which experienced a long tenure on the *New York Times* best-seller list. The book is the story of four mice that live in a maze and search for cheese. As the cheese supply dwindles, Hem and Haw become panicky, angry, and resigned. Sniff and Scurry begin a remarkable journey of change that leads them to even more and better-tasting cheese—besides leading to the book's key message. On the walls of their labyrinth this pair of mice write what they've learned in their adventure for the benefit of other mice—and, of course, for the reader.[33] Living in the postmodern world makes one feel on many days, as though someone has moved the church's cheese. We run the same gamut of emotions as do the mice in the story, feelings that can range from excitement to depression. A pastor's ability to create a an environment ready for change, to lead the change process successfully, and to anchor the change in the congregation's culture—that gift embodies one of the most important skill sets needed for the 21st century.

For my great-grandparents, change was slow. They invented the car. For my grand-parents, change was a little faster. They invented the television. For my parents, change has been rapid. They invented the computer. But for my generation, change is constant. We don't have time to think about it.[34]

This comment by a 19-year-old man in Newberg, Oregon, reflects the dramatic degree of change occurring in our lifetime. Change is constant. It's no wonder that so many parishioners resist change. Or do they? The U.S. Congregational Life Survey learned that 61 percent of all worshipers believe their congregation is always willing to try something new.[35] You may be thinking, "But none of them are in *my* congregation!" Well, willingness and readiness for change are two entirely different things. Pastors need to understand why change is so difficult for people, and to prepare themselves to be effective leaders of change.

One way pastors equip themselves is by reading some of the excellent books on change in both religious and secular markets. One of my favorites is Ronald Heifetz's *Leadership Without Easy Answers*. Heifetz describes two basic kinds of change—technical and adaptive. Technical, or incremental, change is required when the direction or resolution is rather mechanical. A problem is identified and one chooses from multiple solutions. Adaptive change is much more complex and challenging. Adaptive change is needed when the problem or situation is not clear-cut, when everyone shares the responsibility, and when everyone learns something new in working through the change.[36] I believe that orchestrating adaptive change is at the heart of the 21st-century pastor's challenge. Because adaptive change is often painted in broad-stroke descriptors—"being vital and effective," "becoming a boundaryless organization," "a contemporary church for a contemporary people"—it's often hard to know when the change has actually occurred. This wave of transition will likely not end in our lifetime. Some changes toward which we work will certainly be achieved; others will not. Some changes will become irrelevant before they are accomplished, and other, more urgent changes will present themselves on the journey. Change is more of a process than a result.[37] The most successful churches will be those that embrace rapid change as a way of life.

Change is usually unsettling. "Behold, I make all things new" (Rev. 21:5). These words of Jesus are comforting when we consider eternity, but we tend not to trust them so much in our daily life. Each person and each organization has a change threshold. For many of us, a little change goes a long way. I myself love the excitement and challenge of change—in everyone but my husband. A standing joke in our family is what would happen to our marriage if he shaved his beard! It is important to realize that when we think about change, we often see it as something that needs to happen in someone else rather than ourselves. It is important to understand that true change generally begins with individuals, not with the organization. If the pastor and key leaders are not 100 percent convinced that change will lead to greater faithfulness on the part of a congregation, change should not be attempted. The pastor must be willing to embrace change personally as well as to lead it professionally. The pastor has to be emotionally and spiritually ready to travel into the unknown and to "get lost with confidence" if he or she is to succeed in leading change in the congregation.[38] Effective 21st-century pastors must also be prepared emotionally to deal with failure—change is hard, and we will not always succeed. It takes emotional and spiritual maturity to recognize and accept this fact. Pastors must be able to cope with their own sense of failure if they hope to help members of the congregations to deal with an unfulfilled dream.

The pastor's first step in leading change includes establishing a sense of urgency. Change for the sake of change is never worthwhile. Members need to understand why this change is essential to the kingdom of God. How will this change move us toward being more faithful responders to God's call? There is a fine line between establishing urgency and creating panic. Urgency produces an environment in which deliberate, planned risk-taking is required. People are willing to change because they know the change will be important for the life of the congregation. In contrast, panic is often unfocused, survival based, sometimes crisis driven; it often happens after a long period of congregational complacency.[39] An effective pastor knows how to build a sense of urgency that attracts wide commitment for change and fosters creativity in members.

Pastors serving in the postmodern world need a solid understanding of change theory. Kurt Lewin, the father of modern change theory, describes three phases of change—unfreezing the organization from its current state, the transition to the new state, and refreezing the organization in the changed state.[40] If only it were so easy! Among the best resources for a clear understanding of the steps for change is John Kotter's book *Leading Change.* Kotter presents an eight-stage process for leading organizational change that is easily understood and applied to congregational life. We need to recognize that although theories about change are helpful, change is always messy. Regardless of which change theory we use as a guideline, change seems never to progress smoothly or in any predictable order. Surprises always crop up along the way. Effective pastors understand this element of uncertainty and are not thrown off course when things don't go "by the book."

Understanding change theory, however, is not enough. Pastors need to understand the emotional dynamics of leading change if they are to minister effectively to everyone involved. Alban Institute senior consultant Gil Rendle calls this "riding the roller coaster" in his helpful book *Leading Change in the Congregation.*[41] This analogy is dead-on accurate. Just as the roller coaster thrills its riders at different points, depending on where they are seated, so change affects members of the congregations in a multitude of ways and at various times as they respond to the change. Traditional pastoral-care skills may not suffice to minister to those who are frustrated that change isn't happening quickly enough or those unable to move through the sense of loss that change sometimes elicits. Change has a cost, and it often includes the unfortunate loss of families unable to embrace the congregation's new direction. Mike Slaughter reports that Ginghamsburg United Methodist Church lost 30 of its 90 families when the congregation began its journey of transformation.[42] Twenty-five years later this excellent congregation welcomes thousands in worship each weekend. Even if the direction of change has been prayerfully discerned, carefully planned, and generally accepted, some people may still be unhappy. The pastor may need new skills with which to bless people and lovingly assist them in finding a spiritual home that will be more responsive and less unsettling to their needs. The pastor must also help prepare the leaders and members of the congregation for the inevitable membership loss during times of change.

Postmodern pastors need also to understand the importance of community and of celebration. Since adaptive change usually takes a long time, it is important to celebrate the small victories along the way. John Kotter calls these "short-term wins." A short-term win has three characteristics—it is visible to a large number of people (the congregation), is clearly a success, and is easily linked to the change effort.[43] If the adaptive challenge of the congregation included being more responsive to the multicultural nature of the neighborhood (an example of a short-term win), 35 Hispanic youth might be coming to the first Christian rock concert performed in Spanish. Short-term successes

- prove that the sacrifices made for the change are paying off,
- provide an opportunity to affirm or reward leaders in the effort,
- help to fine-tune the vision or strategies for change,
- demonstrate to resisters or cynics that the change can be successful,
- keep the leadership team on track, and
- build momentum for what is truly possible.[44]

Wise pastors create opportunities to continue unifying the church around the changes while building community through such celebrations.

When pastors are engaged in executing a plan for change, their priorities will also change. Review committees must take this factor into consideration in evaluating a pastor's performance. It is impossible to add the new tasks of leading change on top of the already demanding tasks of daily ministry. Some duties will need to be eliminated or reassigned to others. The review process is a wonderful opportunity to discuss any adjustments in the pastor's responsibilities and how those changes will be communicated to the congregation.

QUESTIONS FOR THE PASTOR ON INTERPRETING AND LEADING CHANGE

1. Have I adequately equipped myself with a working knowledge of change theory?
2. Do I feel competent in my diagnostic and planning skills for leading change?
3. Am I able to create a sense of urgency that will motivate our congregational leaders to consider the need for change?
4. Have I equipped the formal leadership board of the church to understand the dynamics of change?
5. Do I build in moments of celebration as we successfully complete smaller steps toward larger change?
6. Am I prepared to minister to those for whom the change, or pace of change, is difficult?

QUESTIONS FOR THE REVIEW COMMITTEE ON THE PASTOR'S ABILITY TO INTERPRET AND LEAD CHANGE

1. How effective has our congregation been in meeting the challenge of change this year?
2. How effective is our pastor in creating a healthy environment in which change can occur?
3. How effective is our pastor in working with others to determine the need for change?
4. How effective is our pastor in interpreting change?
5. How effective is our pastor in caring for the congregation as members respond to change?

Characteristic 6: The Ability to Promote and Lead Spiritual Formation for Church Members

> In contemporary American culture, the religions are more and more treated as just passing beliefs.... Through all of this trivializing rhetoric runs the subtle but unmistakable message: pray if you like, worship if you must, but whatever you do, do not on any account take your religion seriously.[45]

According to an article in Louisville Presbyterian Seminary's magazine, *The Mosaic*, the majority of Presbyterian Church (U.S.A.) congregations seeking a pastor will list "spiritual formation" second only to worship leadership, but most of them would not be able to explain what they mean.[46] Sometimes the congregation itself can't agree on a definition. We do know, however, that the word *spirituality* is everywhere. One of the characteristics of the postmodern world is the freedom to explore in the spiritual realm. Believers and nonbelievers alike are doing everything from frequenting New Age bookstores to surfing the Internet seeking direction for their spiritual lives. Most mainline pastors report with sadness, however, that traditional programs such as Sunday school continue to decline. Perhaps that's because we still operate on the rational, modern-era belief that spirituality as something we can "teach" people. Loren Mead, in his book *Five Challenges for the Once and Future Church,* calls for a journey toward "passionate spirituality," one in which individuals connect their knowledge of God with their *experience* of God.[47] Perhaps postmodern people don't find their experience validated by the traditional church educational program.

For Mead, the mainline church has much to learn from the charismatic arm of Christianity. He describes traditional spirituality as having form, structure, and a rational base that is disciplined, deep, and private. Passionate spirituality, on the other hand, comes out of direct relationship with God, is free-flowing, emotional, spontaneous, and communal.[48] Because the world in which we live is more mysterious and unexplainable than we once thought, people are seeking a spirituality that matches—one that does not prescribe six steps to holiness or limit religious experience to an hour on Sunday morning.[49]

Such a spirituality might focus on the transcendence of God as well as the incarnational God, sermons that raise questions as much as provide answers, or more frequent opportunities for silent retreats or other spiritual disciplines that connect members with the powerful presence of a God we can never fully understand.

The effective 21st-century pastor understands the longing of parishioners to know God in a deeper and more meaningful way. Responding to this challenge is daunting—less than half of worshipers spend time each day in prayer or private devotional activities.[50] One criterion for assessing parishes and congregations used in the Parish/Congregation Study to identify 100 excellent parishes was "emphasis on true spirituality and a deep relationship with God."[51] Reintroducing such traditional practices as prayer, Bible study, small groups, and discernment of spiritual gifts can give them new meaning in the postmodern era. Perhaps the years of assuming that people understood these resources have come to an end. A pastor's efforts to teach about these ancient practices and to encourage participation in small study groups will encourage members' spiritual work and may actually be welcomed by those who are not now engaged in such practices.

Carol Childress, editor of Leadership Network's online newsletter *Explorer*, prefers to call the process of spiritual formation for believers "disciple making."[52] Childress pointed me to the ministry of Prince of Peace Lutheran Church in Burnsville, Minnesota, mentioned previously in this book, as an example of effective work in this area. "Everything that happens at Prince of Peace grows out of our commitment to the 'Marks of Discipleship,'" said Pastor Mike Foss in an interview. Foss's preaching, his approach to pastoral care, and his work toward maturing Christians all grow out of the covenant that members are asked to consider. The goal for every member is to

- pray daily,
- worship weekly,
- read the Bible daily,
- serve at and beyond Prince of Peace,

- relate to others to encourage spiritual growth, and
- give a tithe (10 percent) and beyond.[53]

Members of Prince of Peace fine-tune the Marks of Discipleship in small groups called Care Ciple (a combination of the words care and disciple). Creating small-group opportunities for Christians, in which they can deepen their faith in the presence of individuals who can know them well, is often a goal in successful postmodern churches. The idea of small groups is not new. John Wesley expected members of the early Methodist movement to be a part of "classes" or "bands," which gathered 10 to 12 individuals for spiritual development and the collection of money for the poor.[54] Today Pastor Mike Slaughter encourages all members of Ginghamsburg Church to participate in a cell group. Cells groups at Ginghamsburg offer a wide range of group options (married without children, single-sex, by age group, "married again," etc.). In smaller-membership congregations where numbers are insufficient for several groups, there may be only one group, led by the pastor or by one of the other spiritual leaders of the congregation.

Teaching people to pray for the first time, or to deepen their prayer life, is also an important part of Christian discipline. Almost all effective 21st-century congregations offer weekly opportunities to pray with a group, online prayer chains, and assistance in finding a prayer partner. Postmodern churches do not see the pastor as the only one capable of leading public prayer. The postmodern church invites lay members to lead in public prayer more often than the pastor.

The Sunday morning sermon is all too often the only occasion for people to learn about the Bible. One way the pastor can make a real impact in congregants' faith journeys is through the teaching of the scriptures. In the life of my denomination pastors were once referred to as "teaching elders." If we are to revitalize our members for this new era of ministry, we must ground them with our road map—the Bible. Pastors can lead Bible studies, train lay leaders to be effective Bible teachers, and offer daily or weekly online Bible studies (a great way to present the exegesis for the week's worship message). The pastor may not be the only Bible teacher but should be considered the primary theological and biblical resource for the congregation.

Assessing the spiritual gifts of members is another important task for the postmodern church. At Zionsville Presbyterian Church in Zionsville, Indiana, all members and seekers are invited to take a spiritual-gifts inventory. Executive Pastor Bob Jordan says, "At Zionsville PC we want to bridge the gap between 'consumers' of church and disciples in the world. We have a team of laypeople who work with all inquirers and who help them connect their spiritual gifts with a ministry team engaged in mission and outreach."[55] Another important task for the pastor, as well as for other congregational leaders, is identifying members within the church who have particular gifts for a church vocation. One strength that has been lost in the transition from the late-modern era to the postmodern is the pastor's challenge to young people to consider a church vocation. Many seminarians in the 1940s through the early 1960s had been tapped on the shoulder by their pastor as seniors in high school and asked, "Have you ever considered going into the ministry?" Today's youth have so many options available that ordained ministry and other church-related careers seem scarcely visible on their radar screens.

At Second Presbyterian Church in Indianapolis, high school seniors are invited to participate in a yearlong theology study seminar culminating in a trip to Greece or Israel/Palestine. This "Footsteps in Faith" program offers the opportunity to talk one-on-one with students who may be open to exploring professional ministry options. Not only young adults have gifts to share, as is evidenced by the trend of second-career seminarians. Most people who eventually end up in a church-related profession were nurtured first in a loving congregation. Pastors and members have a joint responsibility to see that such opportunities are regularly put before the church.

A central part of postmodern ministry involves identifying the pastor as the lead but not sole teacher of the faith; providing opportunities for spiritual growth, both individual and corporate; recognizing various levels of faith development and planning programs accordingly, and recognizing and developing the spiritual gifts of each member.

For Christians, spirituality is all about taking your religion seriously. It is about our relationship, both personal and corporate, with a living God and Savior. Eugene Peterson describes spirituality as "living fully and well" and notes, "Spirituality is never a subject that we can attend to as a thing-in-itself. It is always an operation of God in which our human lives are pulled into and made participants in the life of God, whether as lovers or rebels."[56] The effective pastor and congregation will make this spiritual growth a top priority.

QUESTIONS FOR THE PASTOR ON PROMOTING AND LEADING SPIRITUAL FORMATION FOR CHURCH MEMBERS

1. Do I provide the opportunity for spiritual direction for those seeking a more deliberate approach to their spiritual life?
2. Is my preaching focused on transforming lives and equipping disciples?
3. Am I personally involved in activities in the life of the congregation that promote spiritual growth (i.e., leading Bible study)? This involvement will vary, depending on the size of the congregation.
4. Does our ministry plan provide for multiple options for spiritual growth, recognizing different levels of spiritual maturity?
5. Do we have a process by which the spiritual gifts of each member are identified and encouraged?
6. Have I identified the gifts for ordained ministry or other church professions in others and challenged them to consider a "call"?

QUESTIONS FOR THE REVIEW COMMITTEE ON PROMOTING AND LEADING SPIRITUAL FORMATION FOR CHURCH MEMBERS

1. How effective has our congregation been in providing opportunities for spiritual growth for the members?
2. How effective is our pastor in encouraging others to engage in spiritual growth?

3. How effective is our pastor in helping members to identify and use their spiritual gifts?

Characteristic 7: The Ability to Provide Leadership for High-Quality, Relevant Worship Experiences

No single area of the church's life is more debated today than what constitutes meaningful, appropriate worship. The "worship wars" continue, well fueled by the energy and the fears of those of us already in the church. Thirteen experts recently surveyed by the Alban Institute agree that no end is in sight—ongoing change in worship styles is a way of postmodern life.[57] Terms like "blended," "multisensory," "postmodern," "praise service," "contemporary," "vintage," and "traditional" replace the previous labels of "first" and "second" service, which usually meant that one had the choice of two identical worship experiences. There is almost as much battle over the name given to these worship opportunities as to the style of worship itself. One of the most fascinating congregations in the presbytery I serve calls its alternative service "Alive Time." I have often wondered what that implies about the second, more classical service. In this book I will not be engaging in this debate. My intent, rather, is to highlight the need for culturally relevant worship that has integrity and speaks to the heart of believers and believers-in-the-making. Frankly, I'm not sure any church today can meet this need effectively by offering only one worship service. If you're a pastor or member of a review committee in a smaller-membership church, don't quit reading! I'll address your concerns at the end of this discussion.

I am a strong proponent for all but the very newest of mainline congregations continuing to offer at least *one* weekly opportunity for worship based on the traditional forms. It would be unconscionable to discontinue forms of worship that have transported so many Christians to the presence of God over the years. I am equally committed to the position that all churches need to offer at least one alternative to that service to meet the highly diverse needs of a postmodern population.

No one congregation, no matter how large or successful, will offer enough worship services to reach every need. The key to planning for additional services is knowing whom you're trying to reach. There are obviously enough unchurched people to go around; the question is, Whom is God calling us to invite into Christ's family through a worship experience?

Churches need to know whom they're trying to reach with a new service. They also need to know what styles of worship are already being offered in a community. Finding the right style and time for a service is a prayerful, research-based process. A community of 30,000 can accommodate only so many services that use movie/video clips in worship or meet around tables rather than in pews. Who in our community is not being served? What style of worship might invite them into a relationship with God? What time of day, what day of the week, and what location should we use? All of these are important questions for the postmodern pastor and the successful 21st-century church.

Sally Morgenthaler, a consultant and frequently sought-after workshop leader, identifies four important elements for postmodern worship in her outstanding book *Worship Evangelism: Inviting Unbelievers into the Presence of God*:

1. a nearness to God (an opportunity to feel God's presence),
2. a knowledge of God (worship . . . centered on Jesus Christ),
3. a vulnerability to God (an invitation to open oneself to God), and
4. interaction with God and with other worshipers.[58]

Worship in the modern era often focused on learning about God. In the postmodern era worship focuses on experiencing God. Postmoderns see worship as a matter of the heart, not the head. The worship format Morgenthaler recommends is one that, through music, art, and story-style sermon, leads worshipers into an awareness of God's presence in their midst.

Contrary to the belief of some, services geared toward new believers are not "baby church." Research shows that these newcomers do not "graduate" and move on to more traditional styles of worship.[59] Successful 21st-century churches know that those coming into the church through a new service will most likely continue with that same service, which must change and grow as those participants develop spiritually. The addition of new opportunities for worship, both for new believers and other emerging constituencies is an ongoing part of planning. Not all of these opportunities need happen on Sunday or even in the context of the church building.

It should be no surprise that Generation X has grown up on bands and singers, not on orchestras or choirs. The U.S. Congregational Survey confirmed that musical preferences are related to age and that two out of three worshipers 40 years and older preferred traditional hymns.[60] For those under 40, organ music is associated with roller rinks and elevators. Music is the single most divisive issue in the worship wars. Yet music remains the most important emotional component in any service. Donald Miller discovered the power of contemporary music to communicate the sacred as he worshiped in the new-paradigm churches he studied.[61] Those challenging the use of today's pop-style music should remember that Martin Luther set his hymns to German drinking songs and that Charles Wesley used simple folk melodies to make his hymns easy for large outdoor crowds to sing. Successful postmodern pastors, church musicians, and congregations will recognize music for the powerful tool it is and will select music that is theologically appropriate but relevant to the age and culture of the people they are trying to reach.

Preaching or delivering the message is second only to music in importance (a comment that will surely horrify readers from the Reformed tradition, in which preaching is considered the most important aspect of worship!). Pastors in the ministry for 10 years or more are only too aware of the challenges of preaching to a postmodern congregation. Preaching from a manuscript is almost a thing of the past. Many pastors even memorize the scriptures for the service so as not to be confined by the pulpit. Biblical storytelling rather than exegesis seems a more effective way of reaching people. Carol Childress of Leadership Network says:

> We are in an era that's moving away from the world of proclaimed truth and into a world of demonstrated truth. Teaching is now happening through relationships and not in classes. Preaching will always be important, but it's moving away from preaching as knowledge imparted and to preaching as a form of communication. This requires a different set of skills; the pastor becomes storyteller who interprets or explains and validates the experience of people in light of who God is. The pastor links the particular person's story to the larger story of God and God's people.[62]

The pastors of postmodern churches whom I interviewed for this book agree with her. Brian McLaren listed the ability to preach in a postmodern format to be among the most important skills a pastor needs today. When asked, "Has the centrality of preaching shifted for you in light of the cultural changes in the church and the world?" McLaren responded, "I believe preaching is still important, but in a new 'key' or 'mode.' Preaching creates a space for community to form; it's not just about teaching information or motivating decisions as in the past."[63]

Mike Foss responded:

> Preaching is still central, but the focus has changed. Preaching has become, for me, more and more about connecting people to a living God and less about preaching a "correct text." I want people to *experience* God in worship. I preach to the gut, not just the head. I now preach to the *whole* person. Increasingly, I will not focus on ideas unless they translate into changed lives. How will my sermon equip these disciples today? This is a quantum leap for me. Seminary doesn't prepare you to preach this way.[64]

The format for worship at Ginghamsburg often calls for presenting the sermon in short segments, interspersed with music or media. Mike Slaughter says:

In preaching, I've probably returned to the basics. Storytelling is my most effective style. I craft my stories around a Bible text and deliver them in a straightforward way. My greatest emphasis today is on the costly nature of the gospel! Many pastors are afraid to preach about the sacrificial life, what it takes to truly embrace God's claim on us. The church-growth movement was right in its emphasis on reaching new believers, but [it] . . . missed the mark by overemphasizing relevance and underemphasizing revolution. I try to preach radical Christianity. What has probably changed most is the reinforcement of the sermon through new methodologies. . . . Media, video clips, interviews, etc., are all part of my sermonic mode."[65]

What these pastors know is that the art of preaching is always growing and changing. Effective pastors are constantly stretching their skills in this area and seeking ways to make preaching powerful and relevant.

Not all effective postmodern churches use movie/video clips and rock 'n' roll bands. Some of them use candles and incense. "It didn't look like a church in there; it looked like a Wal-Mart." This comment about a new state-of-the art church building was made in a group of young adults who went on to say that they loved architecture that shows a respect for God: "Gothic cathedrals are very cool!"[66] This viewpoint should be a comfort to congregations housed in traditional buildings. This sense of aesthetics extends to some aspects of worship as well. Worship modeled on the French Catholic Taizé service, full of reflective, chantlike music and the use of dim lighting or darkness, is gaining popularity with the under-40 crowd. The Institute for Worship Studies in Wheaton, Illinois, conducted a survey of 176 young adults in their 20s from 38 states and 41 denominations. They discovered that the top 10 elements identified as "very important to me" in a church service included an encounter with God, depth and substance, and more frequent communion. Silence in worship, a more contemplative style, and an experience of community were all in the top 10 of the "very important."[67]

Smaller-membership congregations with at least 75 participants in worship should consider adding a second, alternative service. It may involve reprioritizing the pastor's work, but the shift is worth it. If worship remains one of the most powerful and successful tools for reaching the unchurched, then a large share of the pastor's time should be spent in this area. Excellent worship is a key to effective evangelism and church growth. It's well worth examining how some of the pastor's responsibilities can be shifted to lay leaders to make this happen. A further suggestion for how the smaller-membership church might consider adding a service is discussed in chapter 5.

Last, but equally important, the pastor cannot neglect those worshipers already involved in the life of faith—worshipers for whom the existing services have great meaning. The demands of planning and leading a new service often take the largest part of a pastor's energy and creativity. The people whom God has already given the pastor to serve deserve worship that has integrity, strives for excellence in music and preaching, and encourages participation of the worshipers. Seeking excellence and maintaining the integrity of the worship experience help create an environment in which new worship services are celebrated rather than resisted.

QUESTIONS FOR THE PASTOR ON PROVIDING LEADERSHIP FOR HIGH-QUALITY, RELEVANT WORSHIP EXPERIENCES

1. Have I participated in at least one continuing education event focused on preaching or leading worship in the past year?
2. Is there sufficient diversity in worship (number of services or styles) to reach both believers and potential new believers?
3. Is our worship service understandable for those with little or no exposure to the faith?
4. Is our bulletin easy to follow, with all congregational prayers and responses printed?
5. Do we have a special service for those who are initial explorers of the Christian faith?
6. Is the music in worship relevant to the population we are trying to reach?

7. Am I up-to-date on generational theory and what younger generations are looking for spiritually and in a worshiping community?

8. Am I willing to reprioritize my pastoral tasks to make room for new services of worship that address new needs?

9. Am I willing to get out of my own comfort zone for the sake of reaching others?

QUESTIONS FOR THE REVIEW COMMITTEE ON PROVIDING LEADERSHIP FOR HIGH-QUALITY, RELEVANT WORSHIP EXPERIENCES

1. How effective is our congregation in providing meaningful worship for current members?

2. How effective is our congregation in providing additional services for potential new constituencies?

3. How effective is our pastor in delivering a sermon appropriate to the worship context?

4. How effective is our pastor in leading a worship team to ensure that music, liturgy, and other worship activities reflect a unified purpose?

Characteristic 8: The Ability to Identify, Develop, and Support Lay Leaders

Postmodern clergy use the scriptures as key guides for their ministry. Two wonderful examples of leadership development come from Jesus and Moses. Moses was wearing himself out doing all the work alone until God reminded him through the wisdom of his father-in-law, Jethro, that others were equally able to bear the burden of leadership (Num. 11:16). Jesus called James and John as the first to join his ragtag group of disciples in Mark 1:19 (also Matt. 4:21). These examples do not imply that the only reason we recruit lay leaders is to assist the pastor Paul says that God makes us all competent ministers of the new covenant "not of letter but of spirit" (2 Cor. 3:6). It is clear that effective postmodern pastors remember that the ancient church was a movement led mainly by the laity and know that each member of today's congregation also has a ministry in his or her own right. In his exciting book *Aqua Church,* prolific author and Drew Theological School professor Leonard Sweet writes, "Leadership is less about employing people than empowering people. Leadership is less about controlling people than releasing them."[68] Helping to bring forth and release the leadership gifts of every participant in the life of the church should be a primary goal.

Many people feel a call to use their gifts in the leadership of their congregation. One of every two Protestants and other non-Catholic worshipers completing the U.S. Congregational Life Survey reported holding a leadership role in their parish.[69] Holding a position, however, doesn't necessarily mean that these leaders are being nurtured in their role. In too many churches the official lay leaders are the warm bodies who are willing to serve. Alan Klaas, sociologist, consultant, and author, confirms that congregations in decline are served by a few, long-term lay leaders. These recycled leaders are burned out, tired but often unwilling to let go of the reins. They are often critical of younger church members who seem unwilling to "step up to the plate."[70] Many of these veteran leaders have dutifully accepted the pastor's request that they serve on various committees, even when they had no particular interest in the work. They expect a new generation of leaders to do the same. Tom Bandy, author and church consultant, calls this obedience form of leader recruitment "raising dogs" when we need to "raise rabbits." Raising a dog requires the control of a central authority. Dogs are trained to obey commands, walk on a leash, and stay within boundaries. Rabbits, on the other hand, are self-starters, exploring randomly and trying to figure out a way to get out of fences that limit their possibilities.[71] It is more challenging to raise rabbits, but we usually end up with more of them! Today's church desperately needs leaders who are self-starters and who have permission to run with their gifts.

On my first trip to Ginghamsburg Church in Tipp City, Ohio, I was struck by a huge wall completely covered with small photographs. "Wow," I thought, "They sure have a huge new-member class!" A closer look provided a different insight. Beneath each individual's name was the following: "DAY JOB: TEACHER" (or engineer, etc.), followed by "REAL JOB: THIRD-GRADE CHURCH-SCHOOL TEACHER" (or media ministries team member, etc.). These were not new members of the church; they were some of the "unpaid servants" (Ginghamsburg's term), the real leaders of the congregation. All members of this postmodern church are seen as potential leaders and are given permission and assistance in finding their ministry niche.

A buzzword in some church circles is "permission giving." I confess that these very words strike fear into the heart of most Presbyterians. Permission giving? For what? And what about the session (congregational governing board)? Can we really trust members to make good decisions on their own? Empowering members to be leaders means freeing them to do the ministry to which they feel called—without waiting nine months for seven layers of approval! Becoming a permission-giving congregation does not mean giving up accountability, but it may mean giving up control. *Control* means that official leaders decide what can be done and who can do it. *Accountability* allows members freedom to do what they feel is important but within the normative boundaries of the values, beliefs, and mission of the congregation.[72] Some churches are even setting aside a portion of their mission money for ministry projects started by members. Only three people have to sign off for the member to put the project on the church calendar and to receive a small seed grant to get it started.

Even our understanding of the identified leadership of the church—the board, the vestry, the session—is changing in a postmodern context. Mike Slaughter found that having a large board of interested but uninformed leaders wasn't ultimately helpful, even when each held a high-profile job in the community. The Ginghamsburg congregation solved this problem by reducing the official board to nine (still in accordance with United Methodist polity) but recruited people who had proved themselves leaders in their secular life and who also demonstrated spiritual maturity. They, along with the staff team, agreed to learn everything they could about the emerging postmodern church and committed themselves to spending at least one week of their personal vacation each year attending a national church training event together.[73] This congregation learned that capable people in the business world might not always be the best leaders in the church world, but that the powerful combination of secular leadership skills coupled with mature, faithful discipleship could result in exciting, creative leadership.

Whether working to encourage members in developing and executing their own leadership gifts or working with the official or elected leaders of the church, the pastor serves as leadership coach. To encourage these outcomes, the pastor can meet with leaders to discuss their ministry, provide notes of encouragement, suggest books, workshops, or Web sites that can assist them. The pastor does not need to have the same skills as the leader to be helpful, and the pastor certainly does not need to have skills superior to those of the person doing the ministry. The pastor does need to be willing and able to make time for leader support.

QUESTIONS FOR THE PASTOR ON THE ABILITY TO IDENTIFY, DEVELOP, AND SUPPORT LAY LEADERS

1. Whom have I nurtured into a new leadership position this year?
2. How have I encouraged new members to use their gifts in the life of the congregation?
3. What leadership training opportunities were provided for present leaders?
4. How many workshops or conferences did I attend with congregational leaders?
5. In what specific ways did I support current leaders?
6. How often did I meet one-on-one with key leaders to offer encouragement and support?
7. How did I fulfill my role as "coach" with leaders this year?
8. How often did I pray for the church's lay leadership team?

QUESTIONS FOR THE REVIEW COMMITTEE ON THE PASTOR'S ABILITY
TO IDENTIFY, DEVELOP, AND SUPPORT LAY LEADERS

1. How effective is our congregation in identifying and developing the leadership gifts of our members?
2. How effective is our congregation in providing leadership opportunities?
3. How effective is our pastor in identifying potential new leaders for our congregations?
4. How effective is our pastor in encouraging and supporting lay leadership?

Characteristic 9: The Ability to Build, Inspire, and Lead a Staff/Volunteer Team

> The future belongs not so much to movers and shakers but to leaders who can work in teams. In fact, the movers and shakers of postmodern culture are teams, which must become the dominant model for ministry and mission. There are no more clergy and laity. There are only ministers.[74]

This quotation from Leonard Sweet sums up the importance of a team approach to 21st-century ministry. Building effective teams doesn't begin with technique; it begins with the condition of one's heart. Wayne Cordeiro, author of *Doing Church as a Team,* describes this heart as "unselfish, authentic and desiring only God's best." It constantly asks the question, "How can I include others?"[75]

Whether a paid staff, a volunteer staff, or a combination of the two, teams live out the kind of community into which God is calling us. When the modern churches thought about teams, they usually connected them with the softball league. The postmodern church thinks "team" as a way of life, doing the daily business of church. Brian McLaren suggests that baseball is no longer the most helpful analogy for "team." Baseball is sequential, with one player batting and then the next batter taking a turn. McLaren thinks postmodern teams are more like soccer or basketball, in which play is constant and the relationship between players vital to success.[76] Presbyterian pastor and author George Cladis uses the theological concept of the Trinity as an example of postmodern teams. Cladis refers to the image used by John of Damascus, a seventh-century Greek theologian who described the relationship of the three persons of God as *perichoresis*, or a circle dance. The Father, Son, and Holy Spirit are engaged in constant movement that implies "intimacy, equality, unity yet distinction, and love."[77] So is a church team constantly sharing leadership, recognizing the gifts of each member; it is based on a love of Jesus Christ and a desire to serve him.

Some congregations have eliminated committees in favor of "ministry teams." We need to remember, however, that if it walks like a committee, talks like a committee, and functions like a committee—need I say more? Teams function very differently from committees. Although a team may have an identified leader, that person's role is to convene the team and then release its members for service. The leader may continue to coach and be available for support, but he or she trusts the team members to fulfill their mission. For example, the first true taste of team common to many churches on the transitional journey to postmodern life is that of the worship team. It is here that lay members are often invited to share their talents in music selection and performance. Perhaps one team member coordinates drama and another designs the visual aids for worship.

Many churches have experienced great success with using such teams. This is a true postmodern team *only* if each member has the same opportunity to shape the feel, flow, or content of the worship service as does the preacher! If the pastor controls the agenda, beyond his or her responsibility for preaching and interpreting the historical perspectives on worship unique to that tradition, then it's just a worship committee with a few talented people included.

Effective teams value diversity, appreciate the leadership role of the convener or team leader without being intimidated by it; develop sensitivity to issues that might arise from age, gender, race, or culture; recognize the unique gifts of each member; and root their work in a common vision. Teams regularly evaluate, giving and receiving feedback as a way of striving for excellence. Team members who are

respected and treated as equal partners will have an emotional investment in the outcome, which then leads to even deeper commitment.[78]
When decision making is in the hands of postmodern teams, they ultimately become more creative.

Many modern-era churches have been blessed with committees
that have naturally functioned as teams. But for churches whose committees have functioned in a hierarchy, where the motivation for pres-
tige or power has been the driving force for service, where members
had to leave the group's work once their formal "term of service" had
been completed, or where only a few did all the work, the idea of teams
will be totally new. I hope it will also be refreshing!

Another place where teamwork is essential is in the staff. One of
the most important tasks of an effective postmodern pastor is building
a staff team. In the very large congregation the day-to-day management of staff may be done by a senior associate or business manager. In
the smaller congregation the staff team may include a volunteer secre-
tary or music director. Whether the church is very large or very small
or somewhere in between, a pastor is always responsible for team development. Kevin Lawson, director of the Ph.D. program in Christian
Education at Talbot School of Theology in La Mirada, California, has
identified 12 characteristic expectations that team members value from
their supervisor (team leader). I have slightly modified them as excellent ways of building strong teams. These are:

- helping the team develop a sense of partnership,
- leading the ministry team in a shared vision,
- building a climate of trust,
- being available and approachable to one another,
- supporting and encouraging each person's ministry,
- caring for the whole person, not just his or her team
  contribution,
- building a sense of healthy loyalty to the team,
- keeping communication open,
- giving and receiving constructive feedback,

- serving as models and mentors to one another in ministry,
- encouraging personal and professional development, and
- praying for and with the team.[79]

To Lawson's list I would add the importance of identifying potential staff members whose gifts and passions for ministry match those of the church.

A good staff is the most valuable tool any pastor can have in ministry. Recognizing that each member's contribution is invaluable to the whole, the pastor can set the tone of the staff as "team." Jim Capps, senior pastor of Southport Presbyterian Church in an Indianapolis suburb, is committed to such team leadership. Working with a consultant from the denominational office, the entire staff, from custodians to pastors, spent an entire year writing a staff covenant that reflected the theological, biblical, and missional basis for their work together. The covenant also included behavioral agreements about how the staff wanted to work together. A small writing team that included representatives from the administrative, programmatic, and pastoral teams brought several drafts to the larger staff table. When every team member could affirm the covenant, a celebration was held, complete with a cake. The covenant is renewed each time a new person joins the staff and is revised yearly. Pastor Capps demonstrated that he knew the importance of building, inspiring, and leading a team by initiating this covenanting process. He did not know the outcome at the beginning, but he trusted that the process itself would contribute to the building of the team—and it did!

Office teams, staff teams, mission teams, prayer teams—teams are everywhere in the postmodern church. The successful pastor will encourage the use of teams and will model healthy team leadership by how he or she recruits, trusts, and supports the team. The effective pastor also demonstrates that he or she can comfortably be a team member when not serving as the team leader.

QUESTIONS FOR THE PASTOR ON THE ABILITY TO BUILD, INSPIRE,
AND LEAD A STAFF/VOLUNTEER TEAM

1. How have I contributed to building a healthy workplace culture?
2. Can the members (both staff and volunteer) of our
   leadership team articulate the core values of the team?
3. Has our team developed (or reviewed) a staff covenant?
4. How often does the staff team meet?
5. How often does the staff meet with the volunteer team?
6. Are lines of accountability clear in both staff and
   volunteer teams?
7. Which of the following components are regular parts of
   team life?
   - Prayer
   - Bible study
   - Opportunity for personal sharing
   - Reflections on our spiritual journeys
   - Critique and feedback (on events and professional
     performance)
   - Problem solving
   - Collaboration
   - Creative brainstorming for new ideas and possibilities
   - Learning opportunities (workshops, conferences)
8. How often do I meet one-on-one with individual
   members of the staff?
9. Are annual goals/plans subject to review by the entire
   staff?
10. What are my hopes and dreams for the staff team in the
    coming year?

1. How effective is our personnel committee (or its equivalent) in supporting the concept of "team" among our staff?
2. How effective is our pastor in building and leading the staff team?

Characteristic 10: The Ability to Manage Conflict

Churches have fights. People get mad. To deny the obvious in favor of some sugarcoated image of Christians is ridiculous. It stands to reason that all pastors need effective conflict-management skills. In matters of pastoral relationships, group decision-making, or theological debate, the pastor may frequently find himself or herself feeling like a referee.

Conflict in the church is not new, of course, Ammianus Marcellinus, the fourth-century Roman historian said, "No wild beasts are so cruel as the Christians in their dealings with each other."[80] Twenty-first-century pastors have an even greater challenge, however, as they respond to conflict that emerges from the difficult transition from a modern-era church to that of a postmodern Christian community. The effective pastor believes that conflict can be energizing and can lead to highly creative moments in the life of a church if managed skillfully. It is absolutely essential for the health of the congregation and the survival of pastors that their conflict skills be sharp and up-to-date. For this reason I encourage ministers to engage in periodic continuing education related to conflict management, understanding the emotional system of a congregation, leading change, and related topics. Congregational studies are revealing more and more about how churches respond to conflict, and effective pastors need to remain on the cutting edge of such knowledge.

In the foreword to *Never Call Them Jerks* by Arthur Paul Boers, author and professor of pastoral care David Augsburger reminds us, "There are no communal conflicts with a single cause, a solitary villain, or an evil person who must be named, neutralized, neutered, or nuked."[81] My 25 years of consulting with congregations in conflict couldn't confirm that statement more. Gil Rendle provides a simple but useful definition of conflict—two or more ideas present in the same place at the same time.[82] The environment, culture, and issues that result in "two or more ideas" can be highly complex.

Over the past 10 years my experience has led me to believe that the fear of change or the absence of skills needed to lead change is the number-one factor contributing to conflict in today's church. I have previously discussed leading change and now address the conflict that often surrounds it.

Rendle presents a helpful description of many mainline congregations in his book *The Multigenerational Congregation*. He describes the composition of established congregations as "bimodal." Bimodal congregations are composed of two groups that often reflect different generations. Sometimes we call these the "old guard" and "new guard" of a congregation. Most of the time these groups are identified by age, but they can also include the dynamics of longer-term members and newer members. According to Rendle's research, these two groups often operate from different value systems. Although they may like each other very much, they often become polarized over important issues of change versus status quo.[83] Understanding these differences and the motivation each group brings to the conflict can be extremely helpful for pastors.

The pastor and congregational leaders become models of how to respond to conflict in the church. This begins with the way we respond to disgruntled members. We are often quick to label people as troublemakers or antagonists when they resist change or fight to preserve something important to them. There are actually very few people for whom abusive or adversarial behavior is a way of life. Most often we're confronted with people who, for reasons we may not easily observe or understand, are frightened or unsettled and so react in unhelpful ways. Roy Oswald believes that every pastor needs a working knowledge of at least one personality theory that can be helpful in relating to these individuals. A broader understanding of the dynamics of human behavior can help the pastor, and other church leaders, in responding appropriately.

Sometimes conflict in a church resides in the staff. Personnel issues can be time consuming for pastors. Effective 21st-century pastors use the gifts of lay leaders for working through difficult staff concerns. Even the smallest of congregations can benefit from a working personnel committee that oversees and recommends policies, conducts regular reviews, and provides support for both paid and volunteer staff. Every congregation should have some form of personnel policy, including a section on grievances (see *The Alban Personnel Handbook for Congregations*[84]). Postmodern congregations consider volunteer positions to be as important as paid ones and often provide position descriptions and review processes for key volunteers. Having such plans for support and review can be enormously helpful in both preventing and responding to conflict. Although the pastor may have a role in all of the above, the wise pastor shares this personnel work with others.

Sometimes the stress of change or the particular dynamics in the congregation go beyond the skills of the pastor or the leadership team. Effective pastors know when to ask for help. Some pastors use a ministry "coach" or seek out the wisdom of a successful pastor they respect to develop a conflict strategy. Some denominational offices provide good counsel and resources for conflict management. In some instances the hiring of a "change" consultant to work with the pastor and congregational leaders can anticipate the conflict points and provide care and response before they become divisive. In instances of serious disagreement, it's a wise decision to obtain the services of a conflict consultant before the growing discord becomes unmanageable.

Congregational leaders, including the pastor, will model for others how to maneuver the treacherous waters of change, a common source of conflict. Pastors can move successfully through change by staying in touch with the "big picture" rather than generalizing the negative response of a few; providing a safe environment where everyone is encouraged to express their views, both positive and negative; and controlling the rate of change to one that is manageable for the majority.

QUESTIONS FOR THE PASTOR ON THE ABILITY TO MANAGE
CONFLICT

1. Have I prepared myself to understand the dynamics of
    conflict in the church (with continuing education,
    reading, etc.)?
2. Do I understand my preferred conflict-management
    style?
3. Is there a group of lay leaders responsible for resolving
    personnel issues?
4. Are personnel practices and policies:
    • written down and available to all?
    • reviewed annually?
    • faithfully implemented?
5. Is there a clear process for resolving differences and/or
    lodging grievances?
6. Do I effectively use the leadership board of the congre-
    gation in resolving conflict issues in the larger church
    family?
7. Do I have a personal "coach" or "mentor" to whom I can
    turn when I am the focal point of conflict?
8. Do I understand the role and resources of my denomi-
    nation in helping to resolve conflict?

QUESTIONS FOR THE REVIEW COMMITTEE ON THE ABILITY TO
MANAGE CONFLICT

1. How effective and current are our personnel policies?
2. How effective are our congregational leaders in manag-
    ing conflict?
3. How effective is our pastor in working with others to
    manage conflict?

Characteristic 11: The Ability to Navigate Successfully the World of Technology

The "message board" on the Warehouse 242 Web site had the following postings on August 4, 2003: a townhouse for sale, a cottage for rent, someone looking for a roommate, a 1998 Honda "in very good shape!" and, with no further explanation, an engagement ring for sale.[85] This online Christian billboard is offered through the Web site of an evangelical Presbyterian congregation that strives to reach those who wouldn't ordinarily be in worship. This church knows that the Internet has become the primary connector for their mission target.

Two generations of Americans have now grown up as part of the technological revolution. The primary culture of the Baby Boomers was television. Generation X has been shaped by the digital world. See, not read, is the code for this generation.[86] Karen Ritchie, author of *Marketing to Generation X,* expands the importance of technology further by saying, "The future is bright for car phones, beepers and pagers, answering machines, computer mails, and fax machines. These are necessities, not luxuries, to Generation X."[87] We should remind ourselves that Generation X is not the "future generation" we're trying to reach; the oldest Gen Xers are fast approaching their 40th birthdays. How much more relevant will technology be for the younger generations coming behind them?

Electronic media has the same impact on the 21st century that the Gutenberg Bible had on the 16th and 17th centuries. "In the twenty-first century to be without digital power and the knowledge to use it will be the new form of illiteracy."[88] Effective pastors in today's world must be technologically literate and know how to encourage their congregations to use technology for the building up of Christ's kingdom. Being techno-savvy involves more than being able to use a computer. It involves seeing e-mail, Web sites, PowerPoint, video clips, and other media tools as additional resources for communication, pastoral care, evangelism, teaching, and worship.

A small survey of pastors on sabbatical indicated that 85 percent checked their e-mail daily. Eighty-two percent said their use of e-mail was increasing, and 91 percent said their work habits had been changed as a result of electronic mail.[89] I experience this shift personally in my ministry as an executive presbyter. Each morning I receive anywhere from 20 to 40 e-mail messages containing everything from clergy consultation to committee business. All of my pastoral letters to clergy and congregations are now done online. Even the smallest and most rural of congregations have access to the Internet. Creative pastors are beginning to find ways of making electronic mail work for them as well. "Younger members of the congregation would rather receive an e-mail from me than a visit," reported a conferee in one of my recent workshops. People do like to receive mail—whether it has a stamp on it or not!

The Rev. Lucia Oerter, pastor of John Knox Presbyterian Church, a small, redeveloping congregation in Louisville, Kentucky, began what she calls "e-votionals" while serving a previous church. Oerter began writing this daily message with a Bible quote followed by a brief personal reflection as part of her own Lenten discipline and to help spiritually nurture those who couldn't make it to regular church classes. She also sent it to a few friends and colleagues as a way of staying in touch. This discipline lasted much longer for her than the original 40 days, and today Oerter has a list of more than 500 individuals from all walks of life, most of whom she has never met, all of whom find encouragement and challenge in these devotional messages.[90]

Any Internet enthusiast who has needed directions knows that MapQuest or one of its look-alike Web sites is the easiest way to get directions. Internet users new to a community or looking for a local congregation are using the World Wide Web for information that directs them to new churches. Savvy pastors and congregations know the importance of a *good* Web site and realize that it can be a powerful tool for evangelism. At www.ginghamsburg.com you can provide your personal profile and be directed to a cell group that matches your needs, or join an international online symposium that keeps you in communication with other Christians worldwide. Many church Web sites allow you to check out the sermon, register for events, or send e-mail to a particular staff member. One of my favorite sites is that of Casas

Adobes Baptist Church in Tucson, Arizona. The church's main Web page (http://www.casaschurch.org) directs the user to click a link to its Gen X community called "The Gathering." This sub-site is designed and managed entirely by the members and staff of the congregation's Gen X worship community. On this site you can enter "God's Storybook," where you're encouraged to submit or read a story of how the power of God through Christ has changed your life or that of someone else. Having a first-rate Web site is a must for postmodern outreach.

We have already discussed the importance of worship that is culturally meaningful. Let me say a brief word about the particular use of electronic technology in worship. Len Wilson reminds us in his helpful book *The Wired Church,* "Having a big screen doesn't mean lowering it for a video clip or a graph of the church financial state, then raising it and returning to the good old days of doing church."[91] No wonder members are troubled by such use; it's distracting to worship! If a blank screen feels "stuck" in the sanctuary with no thought given to aesthetics, it's probably "stuck" in the service as well. Much thought and planning need to go into the use of electronic imagery in worship.

Today, Ginghamsburg Church is probably one of the most sophisticated users of technology in worship, but even it had a rough start. Pastor Mike Slaughter reports that for the first six months the congregation was lucky if the presentation was in focus. People resisted the change and commented, "This doesn't seem like Ginghamsburg Church anymore. It looks like a slick production" and "We've changed. We are not committed to the same truths anymore!" The Ginghamsburg staff and volunteer media team continued to learn and experiment with what makes for effective use of media images in worship. Fortunately for us, they share what they've learned by sponsoring yearly conferences for other churches on how to use media in worship. Worship at Ginghamsburg did change, but the church also remained true to the unchangeable core value—"Unchurched people matter to God!"[92] The struggle was worth it because today Ginghamsburg offers five celebration services weekly, reaching more than 5,000 people.

Pastors and other worship leaders who know little about the use of PowerPoint or video clips, take heart. Almost any 14-year-old in the church can teach you. In fact, Pastor Eric Lohe of Crossroads Community Church in Westfield, Indiana, has used youth as a key part of his media worship team. This new church development, which still meets in a local public school, always sets up for worship on Saturday afternoon. On one such occasion the pastor noticed a junior-high-age boy hanging around the doorway. "What are you doing in here?" the boy asked. When the pastor explained that he was setting up a media presentation for Sunday's service, the curious teenager stepped in to learn more. That young man, previously unchurched, began running the projector for worship and brought his parents into the church as well.

Even the smallest of church offices should have good electronic technology. At a minimum this includes a good computer, a telephone-answering program, and Internet access. More and more pastors are using the Internet for research and sermon preparation. It is important for the church office to be connected to the Internet. This connection allows the pastor to work in the church office as well as in a home study. Many churches are now providing the previously mailed newsletter online or keeping parishioners linked through chat rooms and online prayer requests. Although nothing replaces a friendly voice at the other end of the line, postmoderns expect to be able to leave a message. Sensitive churches know that listening to a long recorded message about service times and special events is frustrating for members and not particularly helpful to prospective visitors who may turn to the Web site for these details. It is much more effective to have a directory of numbers available for all information including service times. Also, "spell the last name of the person to whom you wish to speak" works fine if the caller knows the person's name. Callers exploring your church may not have a clue who the pastor is—it's better to have your message say, "For Pastor Sorenson, push 1." Remember, technology is here to serve members and nonmembers alike. You *can* make it work for everyone!

Jesus had a marketplace philosophy; he walked where the average person walked. He reached all people in the culture, regardless of where they were socially or economically. The marketplace in Jesus' day was the well at the center of town. Technology forms a huge part of today's cultural marketplace. The core values and purpose of the church do not change, but the way we communicate them must.[93] Twenty-first-century pastors and churches must walk into the new marketplace bravely and with confidence that God can use even these secular tools in creative and life-giving ways.

QUESTIONS FOR THE PASTOR ON THE ABILITY TO NAVIGATE
SUCCESSFULLY THE WORLD OF TECHNOLOGY

1. Am I proficient in basic computer skills?
2. Do I use e-mail as a regular way of communicating?
3. Does our church have an up-to-date Web site?
4. Am I proficient in the use of PowerPoint (or similar software) as an educational tool and worship resource?
5. Are the pastor's Sunday sermons available online?
6. Do I have denominational resources and other ministry aids marked in my Web browser for quick reference?
7. Do I have a clear understanding of the appropriate user of technology in the performance of pastoral care (use of e-mail or Web site, etc.)?
8. Does the church office have voice-messaging capability?
9. Does the recorded message give an option for worship service information, rather than subjecting all callers to a long recorded monologue?

QUESTIONS FOR THE REVIEW COMMITTEE ON THE ABILITY TO
NAVIGATE THE WORLD OF TECHNOLOGY

1. How effective is our church in the use of technology (voice mail, Web site, electronic communications, PowerPoint or similar software, etc.)
2. How effective is our pastor in the use and promotion of technology for our ministry?

Characteristic 12: The Ability
and Desire to Be a Lifelong Learner

"It takes all the running you can do to keep in the same place. If you want to get somewhere else, you must run at least twice as fast as that!" This declaration by the Queen of Hearts in Lewis Carroll's beloved book *Alice in Wonderland* pretty much sums up 21st-century life. Unfortunately it also can sum up the challenge of ministry. Twenty-first-century pastors need to run smarter, not faster. The key to working smarter may lie in how they approach learning. "In times of change, learners inherit the earth, while the learned find themselves beautifully equipped to deal with a world which no longer exists."[94] Because change is ongoing, learning needs to be ongoing as well. Even the best of seminaries cannot adequately prepare pastors for more than the first few years of service.

Most pastors think of learning as something *formal*. The modern world trained us to think about learning in a classroom. Most pastors have study-leave time and money and use it to attend conferences, workshops, or conventions. Some pastors return to seminary for short courses. Most effective clergy do some formal continuing education yearly. Presenting a plan for such study to the church board is one way in which the lay leaders of the congregation can partner with the pastor in strengthening skills or developing new ones. It's also a way that lay leaders encourage the pastor to take the time for periodic "retooling."

Formal learning, however, does not have sole dominion in the postmodern world. Learning here takes place in many other ways. In addition to reading books directed toward the professional practice of ministry, effective postmodern pastors read a broad spectrum of literature and periodicals that help them know the world they're trying to reach. At the time I'm writing, such magazines as *Wired* and *Fast Company* are excellent sources of what's happening in the culture. Many creative pastors set aside a portion of each day to visit certain Web sites that provide articles, ideas, and resources for ministry. I have been a longtime advocate for *The New York Times Book Review* as an excellent summary of secular books, both fiction and nonfiction, which are surely being read by some members of our congregations. I regularly encourage pastors to go to the movies—art always mirrors the culture, for better or worse, and gives us insight into the people we're trying to reach. Movies and novels provide a wealth of sermon material. Pastors who regularly use electronic media in their ministry have trained themselves to "watch" for particular clips that might be useful in illustrating theological issues or raising questions. Television is much maligned in some circles, and some clergy almost boast about not watching it. It's true that there's a lot of bad TV out there. On the other hand, churched and unchurched people alike are watching everything from reality shows to the most current police drama. How can a pastor be effective if he or she has no idea what parishioners are viewing on a regular basis? Nothing catches the listener's attention more than having the pastor refer to last week's episode of a popular show to make an ethical point! Learning isn't limited to the classroom, and learning "smart" means using every experience as a potential tool for ministry.

Each summer I'm privileged to serve as co-facilitator of the Clergy Development Institute, a 10-day intensive program for pastors, sponsored by the Alban Institute. Many of the pastors attending this event are beginning or ending a sabbatical. Sabbaticals are not long clergy vacations. They are an opportunity for renewal and a wise investment on everyone's part. In the introduction to *Clergy Renewal: The Alban Guide to Sabbatical Planning,* the authors list six reasons why churches should encourage their pastor to take a sabbatical:

1. It provides the pastor with a time of spiritual refreshment.
2. It provides the pastor time to develop fresh skills and refocus ministry.
3. It helps prevent pastoral burnout.
4. It can enhance clergy vitality, which renews the congregation.
5. It provides time to strengthen the clergy family through rest and family activities.

6. It encourages laity to exercise new gifts of leadership in the pastor's absence.[95]

Creating intentional space for both the formal and informal learning that can come from an extended period of rest, renewal, and study is not just a gift to the pastor but also an insurance policy that the congregation will be well served in the future.

Effective postmodern churches can be led only by pastors who are lifelong learners. These pastors, in turn, help the congregation to become a learning community as well. Time and money are small costs for such a premium return.

QUESTIONS FOR THE PASTOR ON THE ABILITY AND DESIRE TO BE A LIFELONG LEARNER

1. Am I a student of the culture in which I live?
2. How many of the following do I do on a regular basis?
   - Go to the movies
   - Read contemporary novels
   - Read secular magazines
   - Listen to contemporary radio stations
   - Watch the most popular television programs
3. Do I read widely in both church and secular publications?
4. In how many professional development opportunities do I participate in a year?
   - One-day events
   - Three- to-four-day conferences
   - Weeklong classes or workshops
5. Do I have learning goals for myself each year?
6. How do I contribute to creating a learning community within the staff, leadership team, and congregation?
7. Do I take a sabbatical every four to six years?

QUESTIONS FOR THE REVIEW COMMITTEE ON THE ABILITY AND
DESIRE TO BE A LIFELONG LEARNER

1. Does the personnel committee (or its equivalent) encourage our pastor to take regular study leave?
2. Does the personnel committee (or its equivalent) engage in dialogue with the pastor following a continuing education experience?
3. Does our personnel plan encourage a periodic sabbatical leave for rest, renewal, and study?
4. How effective is our pastor in presenting a plan for a study leave each year?
5. How effective is our pastor in demonstrating his or her most current engagement with the world of culture, ideas, and theology through sermons, teaching, and so forth?

Nothing Lasts Forever

These 12 characteristics present a snapshot of what I believe makes for effective pastoral leadership—today. It is my hunch that these will hold true for a significant portion of this beginning chapter of life in the postmodern church. But these characteristics will not last forever. Just as the world is changing, so will the challenges of ministry change. I would encourage readers to continue to ask their own questions about what makes for faithful leadership in addition to what's presented here. The instruments designed for this book can and should be adapted to include new ideas. Use them as templates and redesign them to meet emerging needs.

NO SINGLE MODEL CAN SERVE EVERY SITUATION; ONE SIZE DOES not fit all. The instruments and processes designed for this book were intended to be revised to fit the needs of the local church using them. This chapter encourages adaptation for the special concerns of the small church and the multiple-staff church, and for reviewing volunteer staff. In addition, we will determine the role of review during times of conflict, the relationship of compensation to review, and the occasions in ministry when reviews are particularly helpful.

Review in the Small Church

"This process will take too much time!"
"We can't find anyone to serve on the review team."
"We love our pastor and don't want to criticize her."

Such responses are frequently heard when a pastoral review is suggested to the smaller-membership congregation. These are natural reactions when almost all church members are carrying several responsibilities and no one wants to rock the boat. The small church deserves an equally high quality of leadership, as well as the same kind of opportunity that larger churches have to ask, "How are we doing on our mission together?" The small church's approach to evaluation, however, may be different.

Nancy Foltz, organizational consultant and author, puts it perfectly when she notes in her book *Caring for the Small Church,* "The small church has a rhythm based more on cycles and swings than on clocks and calendars."[1] Perhaps that's because the small church is really more organic than organizational. The small church's vitality and viability depend on relationships. Anthony Pappas, an author and frequent teacher about the small church, prefers to describe life in the small congregation as a "folk society."[2] Pappas further describes the small church as having distinctive qualities and attitudes. He sees it as a stable rather than changing organization that tends to replicate, not rethink, its previous patterns of behavior. The typical small church sees more of what has been than it does of what might be. Rationally defined goals and strategies are never as important as relationships and habits, especially good habits that have proved effective over the years. The small church lives on the basis of relationship rather than task.[3] The relationship with the pastor is at the center of congregational life, and when that relationship is perceived as good, people may not see any value to conducting a formal pastoral review. So leaders of small churches ask, "Why go to all this trouble if things are going just fine? What if we conduct this review and we hurt the pastor's feelings?"

The idea of a pastoral review is best received if it comes at the pastor's request. If initiated by someone else, it needs the pastor's full endorsement, or it simply won't happen. Even then, getting a review team together may present a challenge. A few small churches will find the process recommended in this book to be helpful in its entirety. Many more will find it useful to pick and choose which parts of the process seem most appropriate or manageable. Pastors may find that completing only the reflection instrument and sharing their self-evaluation and action plan with the church board works best in their setting. Since many clergy are their own hardest critics, the pastor should be prepared for someone to say, "Pastor, you sell yourself short on that one. You've done a great job in supporting leaders." Remember that in relational congregations, it's hard to give critical feedback if the relationship is basically good. If the pastor wants to use the feedback group, it's likely to be less formal in nature. Sharing the plan with a few trusted members one-on-one may get the same desired results as those received from a feedback group. Pastors of small churches may wish to simplify the review and action plan by conducting it slowly. This approach might focus on three or four characteristics at a time rather than all 12 at once. The church should be free to experiment with the process to find what's best for its needs.

The 12 characteristics for effective 21st-century pastors discussed in this book may also be adjusted to fit the environment and nature of the smaller-membership church. One word of caution: Do not sell the small church short. Each of the characteristics needs to be present to some degree for the pastor to be effective in a postmodern world. The pastor or congregation may not embrace everything in each characteristic, and ministry may not be carried out the same way as in larger churches, but the characteristics are still important. For instance, alternative worship in a small rural congregation may be a Sunday evening country-western service conducted quarterly. Smaller-membership churches may not have a Web site but may use e-mail as an effective way to get the prayer chain going.

Whitelick Presbyterian Church sits between the towns of Brownsburg and Avon, Indiana. Pastor Joy Bilger Goehring is blending the proposed tasks of "developing and supporting leaders" with that of "leading spiritual formation for church members" by inviting six leaders in the congregation into a small group for prayer and Bible study. At first, rumblings went through the church that Pastor Goehring was holding some "secret" meetings. She lovingly dispelled this rumor by telling the congregation that she was working with these six leaders to help them become stronger spiritual guides for the congregation.

She told congregants what went on in the meetings and added that additional spiritual-formation groups would be offered in the future.[4] The small-church pastor can focus on the characteristics in ways that match a particular setting.

The Multiple-Staff Review

Can this model be effective for review of associate pastors as well as senior pastors? You bet—with some modifications. With the exception of the occasional generalist, most associate pastors have a portfolio position—youth ministry, outreaches, or missions, for example. Even with a specialized focus, however, they remain part of the team that works toward implementing the overall vision and mission of the congregation. Associate pastors need to maintain personal, professional, and spiritual balance. They need to be able to guide a transformational faith experience. They certainly need to be able to interpret and lead change. The questions in the instrument "Reflecting on Ministry—An Associate Pastor's Personal Evaluation," found in appendix C, includes the same 12 characteristics with only minor revisions to make it more usable for review of the associate. Note that the instrument presented here cannot address the unique tasks of a portfolio position. The review committee should add specific questions to the instrument, based on the associate pastor's position description, *before* the review process begins. Note also that the questions about the congregation's effectiveness in each area are *not* included in the instrument "A Personnel Committee's Evaluation of the Associate Pastor" in appendix D. It is assumed that these questions will be addressed in the senior pastor's review.

In multiple-staff ministries the staff team may to serve as a second feedback group. It should not replace the small group of trusted members, but the staff members can serve as a forum for the pastor to further refine the action plan and, if trust is high, his or her self-evaluation. The senior pastor sets the tone by sharing first. In staff teams that are newly formed or whose trust is being rebuilt following conflict, talking about the self-evaluations with the staff team may be too threatening. In these instances it may be best to disclose only the action plan of each pastor.

Some ministry teams find value in approaching the review process as a form of accountability to one another. George Cladis identifies three benefits for teams that discuss their action plans:

- understanding how their individual contributions fit into the total movement toward the church's mission,
- providing an opportunity to ask how the unique gifts of each person contribute to the team effort, and
- providing the opportunity to form clear team expectations of one another as they pursue the church's vision.[5]

Feedback from peers, including the team leader (who is often the senior pastor), can be helpful if everyone engages in the process. Kevin Lawson suggests four guidelines for providing constructive feedback.

1. Feedback should be given on a regular basis, not just at an annual performance review.
2. Start with the associate's self-evaluation and then give your perspective.
3. Focus first and foremost on the strengths, gifts, and ministry accomplishments; then gently tackle one or two growth areas at a time.
4. Make sure that feedback focuses on their ministry efforts and strategies, not just on the end results. Circumstances outside their control may have influenced the final outcome.[6]

Reviewing Volunteer Staff

In a growing number of churches, members are becoming part of a volunteer staff. This is especially true in churches averaging 40 to 60 participants in worship. In these smaller-membership congregations, a team of three to five lay members may serve in partnership with an ordained pastor.[7] Whether they coordinate the worship team or direct senior activities, these individuals are a valuable part of the staff team. We are often hesitant to discuss reviews with these servants because (1) they aren't being paid, and (2) they're members of the church. Neither is a valid reason for not affording them the same opportunity for feedback and planning that others receive. Neglecting to review their ministry may send an unintentional message that the work they do is not as important as that of a professional staff member. Providing an annual time to reflect on their work may also head off future problems in performance. In my reading and interviews for this book, I did not encounter a single congregation that was currently providing such a review. Since most of the pastors interviewed expressed interest in finding a way to review volunteer staff, I have designed a model, found in appendix E. It is less comprehensive than the one recommended for pastoral review but still reflects on the 12 characteristics important for 21st-century ministry. Like all other instruments in this book, it can be easily modified.

The Review Is Not a Weapon

As mentioned earlier, some congregations don't want to "rock the boat" by conducting a large-scale review of their pastor's ministry. If things are going smoothly, the great temptation is to leave well enough alone. When congregations and pastors don't engage in regular review, they are vulnerable to what Gil Rendle calls "review by complaint."[8] This phenomenon occurs when review committees don't have clear standards for conducting the evaluation. They simply ask, "Are there any complaints?" and if the answer is yes, then they conduct a review. Review committees in postmodern congregations understand that complaints are normal and that change will often bring discomfort. Regular review provides healthy opportunities for concerns to be expressed, treated with respect, and responded to when warranted. Complaints do not necessarily signal that the ministry is doomed or that the congregation is on the edge of the abyss.

Sometimes the church will demand a review of the pastor when issues are deeply dividing the congregation or when conflict erupts between the pastor and congregational members or leaders. This is absolutely the worst time to conduct a review! The evaluation and feedback are so colored by the current tension that honest and constructive responses are almost impossible to obtain. People who love the pastor may pass over aspects of ministry that could be improved for fear their comments might be misused. People who dislike the pastor will avoid saying anything positive for fear it might weaken their position. Although the pastor's role in any conflicted situation must certainly be addressed, a formal evaluation is not the best way of gathering information about what's going on. Congregations are better served by securing the services of a conflict consultant through their denominational offices or organizations such as the Alban Institute than by trying to prove "who's right" about the pastor through a quickly thrown-together review. Of course, the best protection against clergy-focused conflict is the regular review process, when concerns can be addressed before they become problems.

The Question of Compensation

In my book *Evaluating Ministry* I make the case against tying compensation to the performance review.

> When a person's livelihood is tied to how well he or she is perceived to be functioning in a particular position, the stakes on the review are immediately escalated. This quite often blocks honest reflection and assessment and encourages the clergyperson and all those supportive of him or her to present the most positive picture possible. The creative examination of what needs to be improved, done differently, added, or eliminated is hampered.[9]

I do not believe in "merit" increases. My theology demands that the church, of all social institutions, provide its servants a fair living wage for work provided. To suggest that if someone works harder, he or she should be paid more implies that the church embraces the secular notion that money is the prime motivator for excellence. My experience with a great many church professionals is that they know they could achieve greater financial gain in a different career field, but ministry is a calling they cannot ignore.

Our goal in the review process is to assist church professionals in doing the most effective job possible, not to tempt them with a monetary reward for what should be expected anyway. Compensation conversations do need to occur. It is here that the pastor and review committee can discuss congregational finances, projected increases in the future, particular ways in which the pastor may request that his or her compensation be divided (for example, a portion designated as a housing allowance), and other financial questions. Some congregations find that conducting ministry reviews in the fall and compensation reviews in the spring is a helpful way of separating these issues.

It's All in the Timing

By now it should be clear that I advocate for regular ministry reviews. I have also affirmed that the full process suggested here may not be necessary for every pastor and church every year. There are times in the life of a pastor, however, when a full or comprehensive review is particularly important.

The review process presented in this book is not intended for someone who has just completed his or her first year of service. The first year of ministry is one of learning congregational culture and building relationships. The first annual review should focus more on that aspect of ministry. Churches wanting to provide feedback on the tasks of ministry at the close of a first year might consider using the form found in Appendix 073 of *The Alban Personnel Handbook for Congregations*.[10] An action plan formed too early in the pastor's tenure may not accurately reflect the congregation's needs or the pastor's role in addressing them. The process recommended in this book is an excellent one for the end of the second year and for successive reviews. Pastors who wait to develop an action plan for at least 18 months will find that the plan is much more grounded in relationship and a sense of where God is calling the pastor and people together. When the review process recommended here is completed at the end of year two, the action plan should definitely be affirmed or further refined by the official board of the church and communicated widely to the congregation. Publicizing the plan sets the stage for both the pastoral relationship and future direction of ministry together. Sharing the plan with others says, "We've gotten to know each other, and now we're off and running."

Another point at which the full review process might be helpful is between seven and 10 years of service. This seems to be a time of personal reflection for many pastors. They often ask such questions as, "Is God still calling me here? Am I in this for the long haul? Am I still the leader this church needs?" Quite often the process of personal reflection leads to a recommitment. Sometimes it leads to an awareness that it's time to consider a new call. The process of personal reflection and feedback may be extremely helpful in this time of discernment. If the pastor feels called to continue service, the action plan may provide just the right vehicle for thinking about the next stage of ministry. If the pastor feels that his or her ministry in this setting is drawing to completion, the feedback group may help the pastor in the discernment process. The action plan developed when a pastor begins exploring a new call or when the pastor begins planning for retirement will be geared toward closure or completion rather than beginning new projects.

A Last Word

Remember Bill and Mary and Kyle and Molly from chapter 1? They actually have much in common. Although separated by generations and eras of American life, both couples sought an experience with God in a place called church. It's true that the congregational form in which Bill and Mary found meaning is being reshaped for this new era by the Kyles and Mollys of the world. But it's also true that Kyle and Molly look for some of the same things in their pastor as Bill and Mary did—someone to walk with them in their spiritual journey, someone they can depend upon to lead their church into God's vision. The truth of the gospel has not changed, but we have. The postmodern world calls out for new and exciting ways of "being church" while holding onto the command that shapes our existence—"Go therefore and make disciples of all nations, baptizing them in the name of the Father and of the Son and of the Holy Spirit, and teaching them to obey everything that I have commanded you" (Matt. 28:9-20).

Being on the cutting edge of the 21st century entails both joys and frustrations. Despite the rather steep learning curve on which most of us find ourselves, there is great opportunity. The mission field is ripe, and our world hungers for spiritual direction. We are not bound by only one way to be an effective church; many shapes and expressions of the faith can be fruitful and meaningful. Most important, God still stands with us ready to guide, forgive, and comfort as we set off into yet one more new direction. Twenty-first-century evaluation is not about looking at shortcomings and failures but rather about learning from them and planning for the next step. Twenty-first-century evaluation is not celebrating successes so that we can rest on our laurels but seeing success as the fuel that moves us on. It's a glorious time to serve the church as pastor, staff, or volunteer. It is my hope that this book will provide a thorough yet adaptable way of thinking about the evaluation of 21st-century ministry. May God bless the Bills and Marys, the Kyles and Mollys, and all those who seek to be faithful in this remarkable postmodern world!

REFLECTING ON MINISTRY:
A PASTOR'S EVALUATION

A

THE FOLLOWING QUESTIONS CORRESPOND TO THE 12 CHARACTER-istics of an effective 21st-century pastor. It is intended for use by the pastor to reflect upon the role and tasks of a leader in the context of the congregation's ministry. Space has been provided for additional reflections related to the pastor's responsibilities.

For those readers who would like to make changes to the instruments for use within their congregations, a Microsoft Word version of the entire "Reflecting on Ministry" resource is available for download from the Alban Institute's Web site, at http://www.alban.org/BookDetails.asp?ID=1809. The instrument is free for those who have purchased this book. Readers will need the book with them to access the instrument.

Characteristic 1: The Ability to Maintain
Personal, Professional, and Spiritual Balance

1. How often do I engage in the following?
   - Personal prayer not related to role or function of ministry
   - Bible study not related to the practice of ministry.
   - A private spiritual retreat
   - The practice of faithful stewardship
2. How often do I participate in worship where I am not the leader?
3. Do I have a spiritual director or spiritual friend with whom I meet at least monthly for prayer and reflection on my own spiritual journey?
4. Do I participate in an accountability/support group other than a ministerial association?
5. How many "days off" do I consistently take each week?
6. Do I take all my vacation? Do I take at least one portion of it in a two-week block?
7. How much time a week is reserved for home life?
   - Four nights a week?
   - Two nights a week?
   - Saturdays?
8. *For married pastors:* How often do I have "date" nights or other regular opportunities for special time with my spouse?
9. *For single pastors:* Do I spend time with friends or other family on a weekly basis?
10. Do I have friends who are not members of the congregation?
11. Do I have a personal therapist or pastoral counselor identified for times of need?
12. Do I have an annual physical?
13. How often do I engage in physical exercise lasting at least 30 minutes?

14. How balanced is my current diet?
15. Am I more than 10 pounds over the recommended weight for my height?
16. Do I take a multivitamin daily?
17. Do I have interests or hobbies outside the church?

ADDITIONAL REFLECTION

ACTION PLAN

Characteristic 2: The Ability to Guide
a Transformational Faith Experience

1. How many new believers have I nurtured into a relationship with Christ in the past year?
2. Do I have contemporary translations of the Bible on hand that I can give away as needed?
3. Do I spend time in locations where I might meet individuals without a faith background?
4. Do I have a plan for developing new believers into mature disciples?
5. How many "mentors for new believers" have I equipped this year?
6. Does our congregation have an appropriate ritual of welcome for new members and a social event to welcome them into the congregation?
7. Do I encourage people new to the faith to invite their friends and family members into the faith as well?

ADDITIONAL REFLECTION

ACTION PLAN

Characteristic 3: The Ability to Motivate and Develop a Congregation to Be a "Mission Outpost"

1. How many adult baptisms were performed in my congregation during the past year?
2. Is the leadership board clear about the target population this congregation is trying to reach? Is the congregation clear?
3. Do I nurture those who have a gift for evangelism through one-on-one coaching or in small group settings?
4. Is there a formal plan for equipping members as evangelists in my congregation?
5. Have I prepared members to place the comfort of new believers above their own?
6. How many times have I preached in the past 12 months on the call to be evangelists?
7. How have we focused on being a hospitable and welcoming congregation?
8. Do we have parking spaces reserved for first-time visitors?
9. Do we have parking-lot greeters in addition to those who welcome at the church entrance?
10. To what extent is our Sunday school viewed as a tool for reaching neighborhood children and their parents?
11. Do our social-action ministries make a statement to the surrounding community that we care deeply for the poor, homeless, and marginalized people in our society?
12. Are these individuals welcomed into our church?
13. How have we collaborated with other congregations that see themselves as mission outposts in reaching the unchurched in our common community?
14. Do we have a plan for assimilating new members into the life of our congregation?

WHEN BETTER ISN'T ENOUGH

ADDITIONAL REFLECTION

ACTION PLAN

Characteristic 4: The Ability
to Develop and Communicate a Vision

1. Do I annually share my personal vision for the congregation with the formal leadership board of my church? With the congregation?
2. Is our vision statement concise and easy to remember?
3. How is our vision kept before our membership (banners, letterhead, hymns, Web site, etc.)?
4. Is there a process of regular review and evaluation for the vision of the church?
5. What percentage of the congregation could articulate the vision statement?
6. How many sermons a year focus specifically on the congregation's vision?
7. Does our organizational structure equip and support the vision statement? Is it easily modified?

ADDITIONAL REFLECTION

ACTION PLAN

Characteristic 5: The Ability to Interpret and Lead Change

1. Have I adequately equipped myself with a working knowledge of change theory?
2. Do I feel competent in my diagnostic and planning skills for leading change?
3. Am I able to create a sense of urgency that will motivate our congregational leaders to consider the need for change?
4. Have I equipped the formal leadership board of the church to understand the dynamics of change?
5. Do I build in moments of celebration as we successfully complete small steps toward larger change?
6. Am I prepared to minister to those for whom the change, or pace of change, is difficult?

ADDITIONAL REFLECTION

ACTION PLAN

Characteristic 6: The Ability to Promote and Lead Spiritual Formation for Church Members

1. Do I provide the opportunity for spiritual direction for those seeking a more intentional approach to their spiritual life?
2. Is my preaching focused on transforming lives and equipping disciples?
3. Am I personally involved in activities in the life of the congregation that promote spiritual growth (e.g., leading Bible study)? This involvement will vary depending on the size of the congregation.
4. Has our ministry plan provided for multiple options for spiritual growth, recognizing different levels of spiritual maturity?
5. Do we have a process by which the spiritual gifts of each member are identified and encouraged?
6. Have I identified the gifts for ordained ministry or other church professions in others and challenged them to consider a "call"?

ADDITIONAL REFLECTION

ACTION PLAN

Characteristic 7: The Ability to Provide Leadership for High-Quality, Relevant Worship Experiences

1. Have I participated in at least one continuing-education event focused on preaching or leading worship in the past year?
2. Is there sufficient diversity in worship (number of services or styles) to reach both believers and potential new believers?
3. Is our worship service understandable for those with little or no exposure to the faith?
3. Is our bulletin easy to follow, with all congregational prayers and responses printed?
4. Do we have a special service for those who are initial explorers of the Christian faith?
6. Is the music in worship relevant to the population we are trying to reach?
7. Am I up-to-date on generational theory and what younger generations are looking for spiritually and in a worshiping community?
8. Am I willing to reprioritize my pastoral tasks to make room for new services of worship that address new needs?
9. Am I willing to get out of my own comfort zone for the sake of reaching others?

ADDITIONAL REFLECTION

ACTION PLAN

Characteristic 8: The Ability to Identify, Develop, and Support Lay Leaders

1. Whom have I nurtured into a new leadership position this year?
2. How have I encouraged new members to use their gifts in the life of the congregation?
3. What leadership training opportunities were provided for existing leaders?
4. How many workshops or conferences did I attend with congregational leaders?
5. In what specific ways did I support existing leaders?
6. How often did I meet one-on-one with key leaders to offer encouragement and support?
7. How did I fulfill my role as "coach" with leaders this year?
8. How often did I pray for the church's lay leadership team?

ADDITIONAL REFLECTION

ACTION PLAN

Characteristic 9: The Ability to Build, Inspire, and Lead a Staff/Volunteer Team

(Note: in smaller-membership congregations the staff may consist entirely of volunteers plus the pastor.)

1. How have I contributed to building a healthy workplace?
2. Can the members (both staff and volunteer) of our leadership team articulate the core values of the team?
3. Has our team developed (or reviewed) a staff covenant?
4. How often does the staff team meet?
5. How often does the staff meet with the volunteer team?
6. Are lines of accountability clear in staff and volunteer teams?
7. Which of the following components are regular parts of team life?
   - Prayer
   - Bible study
   - Opportunity for personal sharing
   - Reflections on our spiritual journeys
   - Critique and feedback (on events and professional performance)
   - Problem solving
   - Collaboration
   - Creative brainstorming for new ideas/possibilities
   - Learning opportunities (workshops, conferences)
8. How often do I meet one-on-one with individual members of the staff?
9. Are annual goals/plans subject to entire staff review?
10. What are my hopes for the staff team in the coming year?

ADDITIONAL REFLECTION

ACTION PLAN

Characteristic 10: The Ability to Manage Conflict

1. Have I prepared myself to understand the dynamics of conflict in the church (continuing education, reading, etc.)?
2. Do I understand my preferred conflict-management style?
3. Is there a group of lay leaders responsible for resolving personnel issues?
4. Are personnel practices and policies
   - written down and available to all?
   - reviewed annually?
   - faithfully implemented?
5. Is there a clear process for resolving differences and/or lodging grievances?
6. Do I effectively use the leadership board of the congregation in resolving conflict issues in the larger church family?
7. Do I have a personal coach or mentor to whom I can turn when I am the focal point of conflict?
8. Do I understand the role and resources of my denomination in helping to resolve conflict?

ADDITIONAL REFLECTION

ACTION PLAN

Characteristic 11: The Ability to Navigate
Successfully the World of Technology

1. Am I proficient in basic computer skills?
2. Do I use e-mail as a regular way of communicating?
3. Does our church have an up-to-date Web site?
4. Am I proficient in the use of PowerPoint (or similar software) as an educational tool and worship resource?
5. Are the pastor's Sunday sermons available on-line?
6. Do I have denominational resources and other ministry aids marked in my Web browser for quick referral?
7. Do I have a clear understanding of the appropriate use of technology in the performance of pastoral care (use of e-mail, Web site, etc.)?
8. Does the church office have voice-messaging capability?
9. Does the recorded message give an option for worship service information rather than subjecting all callers to a long recorded monologue?

ADDITIONAL REFLECTION

ACTION PLAN

Characteristic 12: The Ability and Desire to be a Lifelong Learner

1. Am I a student of the culture in which I live?
2. How many of the following do I do on a regular basis?
   - Go to the movies
   - Read contemporary novels
   - Read secular magazines
   - Listen to contemporary radio stations
   - Watch the most popular television programs
3. Do I read widely in both church and secular publications?
4. In how many professional development opportunities do I participate in a year?
   - One-day events
   - Three- or four-day conferences
   - Weeklong class or workshop
5. Do I have learning goals for myself each year?
6. How do I contribute to creating a learning community within the staff, leadership team and the congregation?
7. Do I take a sabbatical every four to six years?

ADDITIONAL REFLECTION

ACTION PLAN

REFLECTING ON MINISTRY:

A REVIEW COMMITTEE'S EVALUATION

THE FOLLOWING QUESTIONS CORRESPOND TO THE 12 CHARACTER-
istics of an effective 21st-century pastor. It is intended for use by
members of a review committee to reflect upon the role of the pastor to
lead and encourage the congregation and upon the role of the congregation to support and respond to the pastor's leadership. The questions are also intended to provide evaluation guidelines for those in the
committee who feel they don't have the firsthand knowledge of a pastor's
duties and therefore cannot judge their pastor's effectiveness.

Please use the following numerical scale in responding to the questions:

4—very effective
3—effective
2—not very effective
1—not applicable

Characteristic 1: The Ability to Maintain
Personal, Professional, and Spiritual Balance

Effective pastors maintain a good balance in their personal, professional and spiritual life. The signs of this balance may include taking days off, taking vacations, spending time with family, and participating in events such as a personal spiritual retreat. A pastor review committee should be concerned about the pastor's overall well-being.

1. How effective is our review committee in encouraging the overall health of our pastor?
2. How effective is our pastor in demonstrating a balanced lifestyle?

COMMENTS

Characteristic 2: The Ability to Guide a Transformational Faith Experience

Successful congregations view evangelism as the responsibility of both pastor and congregation. The pastor serves as an evangelist through preaching, teaching, and direct contact with new believers. The pastor also provides opportunity for new believers to mature in their faith.

1. How effective has our church been in reaching new believers this year?
2. How effective has our pastor been in leading new believers into active faith involvement?

COMMENTS

Characteristic 3: The Ability to Motivate and
Develop a Congregation to Be a "Mission Outpost"

Successful congregations understand themselves as "mission outposts" to an unchurched culture. The effective pastor's role is to equip members for successful outreach. He or she does this by coaching, motivating, and encouraging the laity in this responsibility.

1. How effective has our church been in equipping its members to be evangelists?
2. How effective is our pastor in preaching and teaching about evangelism?
3. How effective is our pastor in supporting members who serve as evangelists?

COMMENTS

**Characteristic 4: The Ability
to Develop, Lead, and Communicate a Vision**

Successful congregations are clear on God's plan for their ministry. The effective pastor, working with congregational leaders, assists in articulating the vision to its members and to those outside the church. The pastor also tends the vision through regular review and consultation with the leadership team.

1. How knowledgeable is our congregation about our vision?
2. How effective is our pastor in communicating the vision to our church?
3. How effective is our pastor in providing for the review and maintenance of this vision?

COMMENTS

Characteristic 5: The Ability to Interpret and Lead Change

Successful churches embrace change in ways that empower ministry and respect people. The effective pastor leads change at an appropriate pace and in consultation with congregational leadership.

1. How effective has our congregation been in meeting the challenge of change this year?
2. How effective is our pastor in creating a healthy environment in which change can occur?
3. How effective is our pastor in working with others to determine the need for change?
4. How effective is our pastor in interpreting change?
5. How effective is our pastor in caring for the congregation as members respond to change?

COMMENTS

**Characteristic 6: The Ability to Promote and
Lead Spiritual Formation for Church Members**

Successful churches nurture and deepen the faith of members. The effective pastor may provide direct leadership for this area or may supervise those who do.

1. How effective has our congregation been in providing opportunities for spiritual growth?
2. How effective is our pastor in encouraging others to engage in spiritual growth?
3. How effective is our pastor in helping members to identify and use their spiritual gifts?

COMMENTS

Characteristic 7: The Ability to Provide Leadership for High-Quality, Relevant Worship Experiences

Successful congregations provide high-quality, relevant worship experiences. The effective pastor assists the church in determining the number of services needed, views worship as another opportunity for evangelism, and is committed to excellence in preaching and music.

1. How effective is our congregation in providing additional services for current members?
2. How effective is our congregation in providing additional services for potential new constituencies?
3. How effective is our pastor in delivering a sermon appropriate to the worship context?
4. How effective is our pastor in leading a worship team to ensure that music, liturgy and other worship activities reflect a unified purpose?

COMMENTS

**Characteristic 8: The Ability to Identify,
Develop, and Support Lay Leaders**

Successful congregations identify, develop, and use the gifts of their
members. The effective pastor supports the leadership of the laity.

1. How effective is our congregation in identifying and
   developing the leadership gifts of our members?
2. How effective is our congregation in providing leadership opportunities?
3. How effective is our pastor in identifying new potential
   leaders for our congregation?
4. How effective is our pastor in encouraging and supporting lay leadership?

COMMENTS

Characteristic 9: The Ability to Build, Inspire, and Lead a Staff/Volunteer Team

(Note: In smaller-membership congregations the staff may consist entirely of volunteers plus the pastor.)

Successful congregations exhibit teamwork in staff relationships. Whether working with a professional or volunteer staff, the effective pastor develops a team whose members' gifts are recognized, their responsibilities clearly defined, and individuals valued and respected.

1. How effective is our personnel committee (or its equivalent) in supporting the concept of "team" among our staff?
2. How effective is our pastor in building and leading the staff team?

COMMENTS

Characteristic 10: The Ability to Manage Conflict

Conflict is inevitable, even in the healthiest of congregations. The successful church anticipates conflict and uses it for dialogue and potential growth. The effective pastor is not afraid of conflict and has equipped himself or herself to manage it.

1. How effective and current are our personnel policies?
2. How effective are our congregational leaders in managing conflict?
3. How effective is our pastor in working with others to manage conflict?

COMMENTS

Characteristic 11: The Ability to Navigate
Successfully the World of Technology

The successful church understands and uses technology to enhance ministry. The effective pastor is knowledgeable in the use of technology for office use, as an outreach tool and in worship as appropriate.

1. How effective is our church in the use of technology (voice mail, Web site, electronic communications, PowerPoint or similar software, etc.)?
2. How effective is our pastor in the use and promotion of technology for our ministry?

COMMENTS

Characteristic 12: The Ability
and Desire to Be a Lifelong Learner

Effective pastors are lifelong learners. A successful church encourages its pastor to participate in a wide variety of learning opportunities.

1. Does the personnel committee (or its equivalent) encourage our pastor to take regular study leave? *(yes or no)*
2. Does the personnel committee (or its equivalent) engage in dialogue with the pastor following a continuing education experience? *(yes or no)*
3. Does our personnel plan encourage a periodic sabbatical leave for rest, renewal, and study? *(yes or no)*
4. How effective is our pastor in presenting a plan for a study leave each year?
5. How effective is our pastor in demonstrating his or her most current engagement with the world of culture, ideas, and theology through sermons, teachings, etc.?

COMMENTS

REFLECTING ON MINISTRY:

AN ASSOCIATE PASTOR'S EVALUATION

C

THE FOLLOWING QUESTIONS CORRESPOND TO THE 12 CHARACTER-istics of an effective 21st-century pastor but have been slightly revised for use by pastors not serving as the senior or lead pastor. It is intended to offer reflection on the general tasks of ministry and to provide an opportunity for additional reflections related to the associate's specific responsibilities.

Characteristic 1: The Ability to Maintain
Personal, Professional, and Spiritual Balance

1. How often do I engage in the following?
   - Personal prayer not related to role or function of ministry
   - Bible study not related to the practice of ministry
   - A private spiritual retreat
   - The practice of faithful stewardship
2. How often do I participate in worship where I am not the leader?
3. Do I have a spiritual director or spiritual friend with whom I meet at least monthly for prayer and reflection on my own spiritual journey?
4. Do I participate in an accountability or support group other than a ministerial association?
5. How many days off do I consistently take each week?
6. Do I take all my vacation? Do I take at least one portion in a two-week block?
7. How much time a week do I preserve for home life?
   - Four nights a week?
   - Two nights a week?
   - Saturdays?
8. *(for married pastors)* How often do I have a "date" night or other regular opportunities for special time with my spouse?
9. *(for single pastors)* Do I spend time with friends or other family on a weekly basis?
10. Do I have friends who are not members of the congregation?
11. Do I have a personal therapist or pastoral counselor identified for times of need?
12. Do I complete an annual physical?
13. How often do I engage in physical exercise lasting at least 30 minutes?

14. How balanced is my current diet?
15. Am I more than 10 pounds over the recommended weight for my height?
16. Do I take a multivitamin daily?
17. Do I have interests or hobbies outside the church?

ADDITIONAL REFLECTION

ACTION PLAN

Characteristic 2: The Ability to Guide a Transformational Faith Experience

1. How many new believers have I nurtured into a relationship with Christ in the past year?
2. Do I have contemporary translations of the Bible on hand that I can give away as needed?
3. Do I spend time in locations where I might meet individuals without a faith background?
4. Can I explain our congregation's plan for inviting someone to explore a relationship with God?
5. Do I encourage people new to the faith to invite their friends and family members into the faith as well?
6. How does my particular portfolio in ministry support new believers in their faith?

ADDITIONAL REFLECTION

ACTION PLAN

**Characteristic 3: The Ability to Motivate and
Develop a Congregation to Be a "Mission Outpost"**

1. How have I nurtured and encouraged those members with whom I work who have a gift for evangelism?
2. Do I bring to the attention of the lead pastor those with whom I work who might be effective evangelists?

ADDITIONAL REFLECTION

ACTION PLAN

Characteristic 4: The Ability
to Develop and Communicate a Vision

1. Can I communicate the vision for mission and ministry of this congregation?
2. What is my vision for the area of this congregation's ministry for which I have responsibility?
3. Have I shared my vision with the staff leadership team? With the lay leadership team related to this area of ministry?
4. Can I articulate how this vision furthers the wider vision of the mission and ministry of this congregation?

ADDITIONAL REFLECTION

ACTION PLAN

Characteristic 5: The Ability to Interpret and Lead Change

1. Have I adequately equipped myself with a working knowledge of change theory?
2. Do I feel competent in my diagnostic and planning skills for leading change?
3. Do I intentionally build in moments of celebration as we successfully complete smaller steps toward larger change?
4. Am I prepared to minister to those for whom change, or the pace of change, is difficult?

ADDITIONAL REFLECTION

ACTION PLAN

Characteristic 6: The Ability to Promote and Lead Spiritual Formation for Church Members

1. Is my preaching focused on transforming lives and equipping disciples?
2. Am I personally involved in activities in the life of the congregation that support spiritual growth (e.g., leading Bible study)?
3. Have I identified the gifts for ordained ministry or other church professions in others and challenged them to consider a "call"?

ADDITIONAL REFLECTION

ACTION PLAN

**Characteristic 7: The Ability to Provide
High-Quality, Relevant Worship Experiences**

1. Am I up-to-date on generational theory and on what younger generations are looking for spiritually and in a worshiping community?
2. Am I able to articulate the differences in our worship services so that I can recommend the service that meets an inquirer's needs?

ADDITIONAL REFLECTION

ACTION PLAN

Characteristic 8: The Ability to Identify, Develop, and Support Lay Leaders

1. Whom have I nurtured into a new leadership position this year?
2. How have I encouraged new members to use their gifts in the life of the congregation?
3. What leadership training opportunities did our church provide for the leaders with whom I work?
4. How many workshops or conferences did I attend with the lay leaders in my area of ministry?
5. In what specific ways did I support the lay leaders of my ministry area?
6. How did I fulfill my role as "coach" with leaders this year?
7. How often did I pray for the church's lay leadership?

ADDITIONAL REFLECTION

ACTION PLAN

Characteristic 9: The Ability to Be
an Effective Member of a Staff Team

1. How have I contributed to building a healthy workplace culture?
2. How have I supported the work of staff colleagues during the past 12 months?
3. Have I given and received feedback in a way that enhances the trust and cooperation of team members?
4. Have I prayed regularly for my team colleagues?
5. Do I treat volunteer team members with the same respect and confidence as I treat paid staff members?
6. Do I participate fully in staff gatherings?

ADDITIONAL REFLECTION

ACTION PLAN

Characteristic 10: The Ability to Manage Conflict

1. Have I prepared myself to understand the dynamics of conflict in the church (through continuing education, reading, etc.)?
2. Do I understand my preferred conflict-management style?
3. Do I understand the personnel practices and policies that specify the appropriate responses to grievances?
4. Do I ask for help in resolving issues before they escalate into conflicts?
5. Do I make the staff team aware of points of conflict in my ministry area?

ADDITIONAL REFLECTION

ACTION PLAN

Characteristic 11: The Ability
to Navigate the World of Technology

1. Am I proficient in basic computer skills?
2. Do I use e-mail as a regular way of communicating?
3. Am I proficient in the use of PowerPoint or similar presentation software as an educational tool and worship resource?
4. Do I have denominational resources and other ministry aids marked in my Web browser for reference?

ADDITIONAL REFLECTION

ACTION PLAN

Characteristic 12: The Ability
and Desire to Be a Lifelong Learner

1. Am I a student of the culture in which I live?
2. How many of the following do I do on a regular basis?
   - Go the movies
   - Read contemporary novels
   - Read secular magazines
   - Listen to contemporary radio stations
   - Watch the most popular television programs
3. Do I read widely in both church and secular publications?
4. How many professional development opportunities do I participate in each year?
   - One-day events.
   - Three- to-four-day conferences.
   - Weeklong classes or workshops.
5. Do I have learning goals for myself each year?
6. How do I contribute to creating a learning community within the staff, leadership team, and congregation?
7. Do I take a sabbatical every four to six years?

ADDITIONAL REFLECTION

ACTION PLAN

Questions Related to Portfolio-Based Positions

1. What were my major accomplishments this year?
2. What were my major disappointments this year?
3. What changes do I anticipate in my area of ministry over the next year?
4. How might others best support me in the performance of ministry?

THE FOLLOWING QUESTIONS CORRESPOND TO THE 12 CHARACTER-
istics of an effective 21st-century pastor but have been slightly revised to apply to pastors not serving as the senior or lead pastor. It is
intended for use by members of a review committee to reflect upon the
role of the associate pastor to encourage and model behavior for the
congregation.

Please use the following numerical scale in responding to the questions:

    4—very effective
    3—effective
    2—not very effective
    1—not applicable

Characteristic 1: The Ability to Maintain
Personal, Professional, and Spiritual Balance

Effective associate pastors maintain a good balance in their personal, professional, and spiritual lives. The signs of this balance may include taking days off, taking vacations, spending time with family, and participating in such events as a personal spiritual retreat. A review committee should be concerned about the associate pastor's overall well-being.

- How effective is our associate pastor in demonstrating a balanced lifestyle?

Characteristic 2: The Ability to Guide
a Transformational Faith Experience

Successful congregations view evangelism as the responsibility of both the pastors and the congregation. The pastors serve as evangelists through preaching, teaching, and direct contact with new believers.

- How effective has our associate pastor been in supporting the evangelism efforts of our congregation?

Characteristic 3: The Ability to Motivate and Develop
a Congregation into a "Mission Outpost"

Successful congregations understand themselves as "mission outposts" to an unchurched culture. Effective pastors equip members for outreach.

- How effective has our associate pastor been in supporting the laity to be evangelists?

Characteristic 4: The Ability
to Develop, Lead, and Communicate a Vision

Successful congregations are clear on God's plan for their ministry. Effective pastors, working with congregational leaders, assist in articulating the vision to members and to those outside the church.

- How effective is our associate pastor in communicating the vision of our church?
- How effective is our associate pastor in sharing how his or her particular area of service fits into the larger vision of the church?

Characteristic 5: The Ability to Interpret and Lead Change

Successful churches embrace change in ways that empower ministry and respect people. Effective pastors lead change at an appropriate pace and in consultation with congregational leadership.

- How effective is our associate pastor in supporting change in our church?
- How effective is our associate pastor in explaining the rationale for change to others?
- How effective is our associate pastor in caring for the congregation as members respond to change?

Characteristic 6: The Ability to Promote and Lead Spiritual Formation for Church Members

Successful churches nurture and deepen the faith of members. Effective pastors provide direct leadership for this area or may supervise others who do.

- How effective is our associate pastor in encouraging the spiritual growth of members?

Characteristic 7: The Ability to Provide Leadership for High-Quality, Relevant Worship Experiences

Successful congregations provide exciting, meaningful, and well-planned worship. Associate pastors may participate in leading worship with other colleagues. Please take into consideration the associate pastor's role in worship as described in his or her position description.

- How effective is our associate pastor in delivering a sermon appropriate to the worship context?
- How effective is our associate pastor in leading public worship?

Characteristic 8: The Ability to Identify, Develop, and Support Lay Leaders

Successful congregations identify, develop, and use the gifts of their members. Effective pastors support the leadership of the laity.

- How effective is our associate pastor in supporting the lay leaders in the area in which he or she serves?
- How effective is our associate pastor in recruiting and developing new leadership for our church?

Characteristic 9: The Ability to Be an Effective Member of a Staff Team

Successful congregations exhibit teamwork in staff relationships. The effective associate pastor participates fully in the team process.

- How effective is our associate pastor in fulfilling his or her responsibilities as a member of the staff team?

Characteristic 10: The Ability to Manage Conflict

Conflict is inevitable, even in the healthiest of congregations. Effective pastors are not afraid of conflict and have equipped themselves to manage it.

- How effective is our associate pastor in managing conflict?

Characteristic 11: The Ability to Navigate the World of Technology

The successful church understands and uses technology to enhance ministry. Effective pastors are knowledgeable in the use of technology.

- How effective is our associate pastor in the use and promotion of technology for our ministry?

Characteristic 12: The Ability
and Desire to Be a Lifelong Learner

Effective pastors are lifelong learners. A successful church encourages its pastors to participate in a wide variety of learning opportunities.

- How effective is our associate pastor in presenting a plan for a study leave each year?
- How effective is our associate pastor in demonstrating his or her most current engagement with the world of culture, ideas, and theology through sermons, teaching, and so forth?

Questions Related to Portfolio-Based Positions

- How effective is our associate pastor in performing the specific duties in his or her position description?
- In what ways does our associate pastor exceed our expectations for excellence?
- In what ways can our associate pastor improve his or her performance?
- Are there areas of the position description that need revision, because of the changing ministry of our church?

REFLECTING ON MINISTRY:

EVALUATION OF A VOLUNTEER

THE FOLLOWING QUESTIONS CORRESPOND TO THE 12 CHARACTER-
istics of an effective pastor but have been revised for use with those
serving as volunteer members of a church staff. This instrument may be
modified by adding questions reflecting the area in which the volunteer
serves.

Characteristic 1: The Ability to Maintain Personal, Professional, and Spiritual Balance

1. Do I perform my volunteer duties within the number of hours of service agreed upon?
2. Do I conduct myself in a professional manner when serving the church in an official capacity?
3. Do I honor my status as a member of the congregation by participating fully in its life, not limiting my involvement to the areas in which I serve?
4. Do I maintain a spiritual life, including personal prayer and other devotional activities?

Characteristic 2: The Ability to Guide a Transformational Faith Experience

1. Am I comfortable talking about my faith with others?
2. Can I direct someone exploring faith for the first time to the programs of my church that might be of assistance?
3. Do I seek out new members of our church and find ways to make them feel included?

Characteristic 3: The Ability to Motivate and Develop a Congregation to Be a "Mission Outpost"

1. Am I aware of the specific population my congregation is trying to reach?
2. How have I been hospitable and welcoming to visitors?
3. Do I invite people to my church and encourage others to do so?
4. How does my area of service help people to be more effective evangelists?

Characteristic 4: The Ability
to Develop and Communicate a Vision

1. Can I articulate the vision of our congregation?
2. Do I have a vision for my area of volunteer work?
3. Have I communicated this vision to my staff colleagues and other volunteers?

Characteristic 5: The Ability to Interpret and Lead Change

1. Do I ask for the information I need to understand the rationale and steps for changes in my congregation?
2. Can I interpret the rationale for change to others?

Characteristic 6: The Ability to Promote and
Lead Spiritual Formation for Church Members

1. Do I understand how my work furthers the spiritual development of members?
2. Do I recognize the spiritual gifts of others and encourage them to serve in my congregation?
3. Do I refer the names of those who may have gifts for professional service in the church to the appropriate person?

Characteristic 7: The Ability to Provide
High-Quality, Relevant Worship Experiences

1. Am I supportive of the variety of worship services offered in my church?
2. Am I familiar enough with each service to make a recommendation to someone inquiring about worship opportunities?

Characteristic 8: The Ability to Identify, Develop, and Support Lay Leaders

1. Whom have I nurtured into a new leader this year?
2. How have I encouraged new members to use their gifts in the life of the congregation?
3. In what specific ways did I support current leaders?

Characteristic 9: The Ability to Be Part of a Team

1. How have I contributed to building a healthy workplace?
2. Do I attend all staff meetings to which I'm invited?
3. Do I comfortably ask questions of others, to better understand their work?
4. Have I shared my hopes and dreams for the staff in the coming year?

Characteristic 10: The Ability to Manage Conflict

1. Do I understand my own conflict-management style?
2. Do I understand my church's process for grievances?
3. Do I share conflicts or tensions with my supervisor or the person responsible for my area of service?
4. Am I willing to ask for help in resolving a conflict?

Characteristic 11: The Ability to Navigate Successfully the World of Technology

1. Am I proficient in basic computer skills?
2. Do I understand the software programs used in the church office?
3. Can I use the Internet for research or communication related to my area of service?

Characteristic 12: The Ability
and Desire to Be a Lifelong Learner

1. Do I have learning goals for myself this year?
2. Do I contribute to creating a learning community within the staff, leadership team, and congregation?
3. What workshops or other programs have I attended that enhance the performance of my volunteer service?

Foreword

1. Gary Stern, "Mainline Protestants Reeling," *The Journal News,* May 4, 2003.
2. Nancy Ammerman, *Congregation & Community* (New Brunswick, N.J.: Rutgers University Press, 1997).

Chapter 1

1. Stanley J. Grenz, *A Primer on Postmodernism* (Grand Rapids, Mich.: Eerdmans, 1996), 11.
2. Grenz, *Primer on Postmodernism,* 16.
3. Mike Regele, with Mark Schulz, *Death of the Church* (Grand Rapids, Mich.: Zondervan, 1995), 15.
4. Grenz, *Primer on Postmodernism,* 9.
5. Walter Truett Anderson, *Reality Isn't What It Used to Be: Theatrical Politics, Ready-to-Wear Religion, Global Myths,*

Primitive Chic, and Other Wonders of the Postmodern World (San Francisco: HarperCollins, 1990), 4, 5.

6. Grenz, *Primer on Postmodernism*, 3.

7. C. Jeff Woods, *Congregational Megatrends* (Bethesda, Md.: Alban Institute, 1996), 92.

8. George Barna, *Boiling Point: It Only Takes One Degree* (Ventura, Calif.: Regal, 2001), 243.

9. Alan J. Roxburgh, *Starting Strong: Five Keys to Discovering the 21st Century Church* (Costa Mesa, Calif.: Percept Group, Inc., 1991), 21.

10. Jane Wagner, *The Search for Signs of Intelligent Life in the Universe,* (San Francisco: Harper & Row, 1986), 18.

11. Brian McLaren, "Why I Still Use the Word Postmodern," http://www.emergentvillage.com/postmodern.htm

Chapter 2

1. Len Hjalmarson and Rob McAlpine, "Postmodern Possibilities—Part 1," http://www.nextreformation.com/html/articles/postmod1g.htm

2. Loren Mead, *The Once and Future Church: Reinventing the Congregation for a New Mission Frontier* (Bethesda, Md.: Alban Institute, 1991), 22.

3. Mead, *Once and Future Church*, 68.

4. Donald Miller, *Reinventing American Protestantism: Christianity in the New Millenium* (Los Angeles: University of California Press, 1997), 11.

5. Roxburgh, *Starting Strong*, 5.

6. Loren Mead, *Five Challenges for the Once and Future Church* (Bethesda, Md.: Alban Institute, 1996), i.

7. Alan Klaas, *In Search of the Unchurched: Why People Don't Join Your Congregation* (Bethesda, Md.: Alban Institute, 1996), 8.

8. Barna, *Boiling Point*, 236.

9. Klaas, *In Search of the Unchurched*, viii.

10. Klaas, *In Search of the Unchurched*, 9.

11. Barna, *Boiling Point*, 236.

12. Klaas, *In Search of the Unchurched*, 4.

13. Miller, *Reinventing American Protestantism*, 185.

14. Hjalmarson and Alpine, "Postmodern Possibilities—Part I."

15. Paul Wilkes, *Excellent Protestant Congregations: The Guide to Best Places and Practices* (Louisville: Westminster John Knox, 2001), x.

16. Paul Wilkes, *Excellent Catholic Parishes: The Guide to Best Places and Practices* (Mahwah, NJ: Paulist Press, 2001).

17. Paul Wilkes, "Criteria for Assessing Parishes and Congregations," the Parish/Congregation Study. Used with permission.

18. Brian McLaren, *The Church on the Other Side: Doing Ministry in the Postmodern World* (Grand Rapids, Mich.: Zondervan, 2000).

19. Barna, *Boiling Point*, 251.

20. Mead, *Five Challenges for the Once and Future Church*, xi

21. Regele, *Death of the Church*, 202–205.

22. McLaren, "Why I Still Use the Word Postmodern."

23. Roxburgh, *Starting Strong*, 21.

Chapter 3

1. Jill M. Hudson, *Evaluating Ministry: Principles and Processes for Clergy and Congregations* (Washington, D.C.: Alban Institute, 1992).

2. Mike Bonem, James H. Furr, and Jim Herrington, *Leading Congregational Change: A Practical Guide for the Transformational Journey* (San Francisco: Jossey-Bass, 2000), 139.

3. Thomas R. Harvey, *Checklist for Change: A Pragmatic Approach to Creating and Controlling Change* (Lancaster, Pa.: Technomic, 1995), 151.

4. C. Jeff Woods, *User Friendly Evaluation: Improving the Work of Pastors, Program, and Laity* (Bethesda, Md.: Alban Institute, 1995), 69.

5. Oren Harai and Nicholas Imparato, *Jumping the Curve: Innovation and Strategic Choice in an Age of Transition* (San Francisco: Jossey-Bass, 1996), 60.

6. Robert E. Quinn, *Deep Change: Discovering the Leader Within* (San Francisco: Jossey-Bass, 1996), 148.

7. Quinn, *Deep Change*, 149.

8. Quinn, *Deep Change*, 150.

9. Thomas G. Bandy, *Moving Off the Map: A Field Guide to Changing the Congregation* (Nashville: Abingdon, 1998), 28.

10. Harvey, *Checklist for Change*, 150.

11. Harvey, *Checklist for Change*, 159.

12. Hudson, *Evaluating Ministry*, 4.

13. Harvey, *Checklist for Change*, 150.

14. Bonem, Furr, and Harrington, *Leading Congregational Change*, 139.

15. Woods, *User Friendly Evaluation*, 69.

Chapter 4

1. Martin B. Copenhaver, "The Good Life," *Congregations* (Sept./Oct. 2001), 11.

2. Gil Rendle, "The Leadership We Need—Negotiating Up, Not Down," *Congregations* (Sept./Oct. 2001), 7.

3. "The U.S. Congregational Life Survey—Presbyterian Panel Version," May 2001 (Louisville: Research Services of the Presbyterian Church [U.S.A.]), 7.

4. Roy Oswald, "The Clergy Life Changes Rating Scale" (adapted from the Holmes/Rahe Scale).

5. Ronald Heifetz and Marty Linsky, *Leadership on the Line: Staying Alive through the Dangers of Leading* (Boston: Harvard Business School Press, 2002), 177.

6. David Wood, "The Best Life," *The Christian Century* 119, no. 6: 18.

7. Mike Foss, pastor, Prince of Peace Lutheran Church, Burnsville, Minn.; interview with the author, Dec. 10, 2002.

8. Willow Creek Community Church, "Seven Values for Leadership and Staff," distributed at Conference on Developing Leaders, Barrington, Ill., 2002.

9. Roy Oswald, senior consultant, Alban Institute; interview with the author, July 10, 2002.

10. "Selected Findings from the National Clergy Survey," Pulpit and Pew: Research on Pastoral Leadership, 4. (Note: For more information on this study see http://www.pulpitandpew.duke.edu)

11. John Esau, "Ten Things I Didn't Learn in Seminary," *The Christian Century* 119, no. 6: 18.

12. Clergy Development Institute, a 10-day annual seminar for clergy, sponsored by the Alban Institute. For more information see http://www.alban.org

13. Foss, interview with the author.

14. Michael Slaughter, pastor, Ginghamsburg United Methodist Church, Tipp City, Ohio; interview with the author, Nov. 15, 2002.

15. Klaas, *In Search of the Unchurched*, 8.

16. "Selected Findings from the National Clergy Survey."

17. Oswald, interview with the author.

18. Brian McLaren, *More Ready Than You Realize: Evangelism as Dance in the Postmodern Matrix* (Grand Rapids, Mich.: Zondervan, 2002), 12.

19. Klaas, *In Search of the Unchurched*, 14.

20. Barna, *The Boiling Point*, 238.

21. Claude E. Payne and Hamilton Beazley, *Reclaiming the Great Commission: A Practical Model for Transforming*

Denominations and Congregations (San Francisco: Jossey-Bass, 2000), 49.

22. Ted Haggard, *Dog Training, Fly Fishing and Sharing Christ in the 21st Century: Empowering Your Church to Build Community through Shared Interests* (Nashville: Thomas Nelson, 2002), 16–17.

23. Michael Slaughter, *Spiritual Entrepreneurs: Six Principles for Risking Renewal* (Nashville: Abingdon, 1995), 124.

24. Zionsville Presbyterian Church, Zionsville, Indiana, http://www.zpc.org

25. John P. Kotter, *Leading Change* (Boston: Harvard Business School Press, 1996), 79.

26. Quinn, *Deep Change*, 203.

27. Miller, *Reinventing American Protestantism*, 14.

28. William M. Easum and Thomas G. Bandy, *Growing Spiritual Redwoods* (Nashville: Abingdon, 1997), 117.

29. McLaren, *The Church on the Other Side*, 152–153.

30. Easum and Bandy, *Growing Spiritual Redwoods*, 117–118.

31. Cynthia Woolever and Deborah Bruce, *A Field Guide to U.S. Congregations: Who's Going Where and Why* (Louisville: Westminster John Knox, 2002), 75.

32. Peter M. Senge, Charlotte Roberts, Richard B. Ross, Bryan J. Smith, and Art Kleiner, *The Fifth Discipline Fieldbook: Strategies and Tools for Building a Learning Organization* (New York: Doubleday, 1994), 299.

33. Spencer Johnson, *Who Moved My Cheese?* (New York: G.P. Putnam's Sons, 1998).

34. Craig Miller, *Postmoderns: The Beliefs, Hopes and Fears of Young Americans* (Nashville: [United Methodist] Discipleship Resources, 1996).

35. Woolever and Bruce, *Field Guide to U.S. Congregations*, 76.

36. Ronald Heifetz, *Leadership without Easy Answers* (Cambridge, Mass.: Harvard University Press, 1994), 74–75.

37. Harvey, *Checklist for Change*, 160.

38. Quinn, *Deep Change*, 11–12.

39. Imparato and Harari, *Jumping the Curve*, 116.

40. Harvey, *Checklist for Change*, 16.

41. Gil Rendle, *Leading Change in the Congregation: Spiritual and Organizational Tools for Leaders* (Bethesda, Md.: Alban Institute, 1998), 105.

42. Slaughter, *Spiritual Entrepreneurs*, 15.

43. Kotter, *Leading Change*, 122.

44. Kotter, *Leading Change*, 123.

45. Stephen L. Carter, *The Culture of Disbelief: How American Law and Politics Trivialize Religious Devotion* (New York: Basic Books, 1993), 14–15.

46. Garnett Foster, "Spiritual Formation: Can We Teach It?" *The Mosaic* (Louisville: Louisville Presbyterian Theological Seminary), 9, no.2 (spring/summer 2002): 9.

47. Mead, *Five Challenges for the Once and Future Church*, 32.

48. Mead, *Five Challenges for the Once and Future Church*, 37.

49. Woods, *Congregational Megatrends*, 91.

50. Woolever and Bruce, *A Field Guide to U.S. Congregations*, 28.

51. Wilkes, "Criteria for Assessing Pastors and Congregations."

52. Carol Childress, director of information for Leadership Network, interview with the author, Aug. 21, 2002.

53. http://www.princeofpeace.com

54. Slaughter, *Spiritual Entrepreneurs*, 73.

55. Robert Jordan, executive minister, Zionsville Presbyterian Church, Zionsville, Indiana; interview with the author, Aug. 4, 2003.

56. Eugene H. Peterson, "Missing Ingredient: Why Spirituality Needs Jesus," *The Christian Century* 120, no. 6: 31–33.

57. Holly G. Miller, "Collision Course? Traditional Worship Meets the Theology of the Overhead," *Congregations* (July/August 2001), 7.

58. Sally Morgenthaler, *Worship Evangelism: Inviting Unbelievers into the Presence of God* (Grand Rapids, Mich.: Zondervan, 1999), 96–123.

59. Dan Kimball, *The Emerging Church: Vintage Christianity for New Generations* (Grand Rapids, Mich.: Zondervan, 2003), 186.

60. Woolever and Bruce, *A Field Guide to U.S. Congregations*, 31.

61. Miller, *Reinventing American Protestantism*, 8.

62. Childress, interview with author.

63. Brian McLaren, pastor, Cedar Ridge Community Church, Spencerville, Maryland; interview with the author, Nov. 13, 2002.

64. Foss, interview with the author.

65. Slaughter, interview with the author.

66. Dan Kimball, *The Emerging Church*, 134.

67. Robert Webber, "Authentic Worship in a Changing World—What's Next?" (Wheaton, Ill.: Institute for Worship Studies), 17. Note: Conference distribution only.

68. Leonard Sweet, *Aqua Church: Essential Leadership Arts for Piloting Your Church in Today's Fluid Culture* (Loveland, Colo.: Group Publishers, 1999), 188.

69. Woolever and Bruce, *A Field Guide to U.S. Congregations*, 38.

70. Klaas, *In Search of the Unchurched*, 27.

71. Thomas G. Bandy, *Christian Chaos: Revolutionizing the Congregation* (Nashville: Abingdon, 1999), 306–307.

72. Bandy, *Christian Chaos*, 252.

73. Michael Slaughter with Warren Bird, *Unlearning Church: Just When You Thought You Had Leadership All Figured Out* (Loveland, Colo.: Group Publishing, 2002), 151.

74. Sweet, *Aqua Church*, 188.

75. Wayne Cordeiro, *Doing Church as a Team* (Ventura, Calif.: Regal Books, 2001), 177.

76. McLaren, *The Church on the Other Side*, 114.

77. George Cladis, *Leading the Team-Based Church: How Pastors and Church Staffs Can Grow Together Into a*

Powerful Fellowship of Leaders (San Francisco: Jossey-Bass, 1999), 4.

78. Miller, *Postmoderns*, 176.

79. Kevin E. Lawson, *How to Thrive in Associate Staff Ministry* (Bethesda, Md.: Alban Institute, 2000), 177–187.

80. Arthur Paul Boers, *Never Call Them Jerks: Healthy Responses to Difficult Behavior* (Bethesda, Md.: Alban Institute, 1999), 1.

81. David Augsburger, foreword to Arthur Paul Boers, *Never Call Them Jerks*, vii.

82. Rendle, *Leading Change in the Congregation*, 21.

83. Gil Rendle, *The Multigenerational Congregation: Meeting the Leadership Challenges* (Bethesda, Md.: Alban Institute, 2002), 38–41.

84. Erwin Berry, *The Alban Personnel Handbook for Congregations* (Bethesda, Md.: Alban Institute, 1999).

85. http://www.warehouse242.org

86. Michael Slaughter, *Out on the Edge: A Wake-up Call for Church Leaders on the Edge of the Media Reformation* (Nashville: Abingdon, 1998), 23.

87. Karen Ritchie, *Marketing to Generation X* (New York: Simon & Schuster, 1995), 157.

88. William M. Easum, "The Convergence of Spirit and Technology" *Net Results* 23, no.1: 25.

89. Survey conducted among participants at the 2003 Sabbatical Grant for Pastoral Leaders Consultation sponsored by the Louisville Institute, Feb. 24–26, 2003.

90. To join Lucia Oerter's e-votionals contact her at luciaoerter@mindspring.com.

91. Len Wilson, *The Wired Church: Making Media Ministry* (Nashville: Abingdon, 1999), 28.

92. Slaughter, *Out on the Edge*, 58.

93. Slaughter, *Out on the Edge*, 57.

94. Regele, *Death of the Church*, 52.

95. A. Richard Bullock and Richard J. Bruesehoff, *Clergy Renewal: The Alban Guide to Sabbatical Planning* (Bethesda, Md.: Alban Institute, 2000), vi–vii.

Chapter 5

1. Nancy Foltz, *Caring for the Small Church: Insights from Women in Ministry* (Valley Forge, Pa.: Judson, 1994), 17.
2. Anthony G. Pappas, *Entering the World of the Small Church*, Revised and expanded edition (Bethesda, Md.: Alban Institute, 2000), 13.
3. Pappas, *Entering the World of the Small Church*, 94.
4. Joy Bilger Goehring, pastor, Whitelick Presbyterian Church, Avon, Indiana, interview with the author, Aug. 22, 2003; wlpres@aol.com
5. Cladis, *Leading the Team-Based Church*, 104.
6. Lawson, *How to Thrive in Associate Staff Ministry*, 184.
7. Lyle E. Schaller, *The Small Membership Church: Scenarios for Tomorrow* (Nashville: Abingdon, 1994), 125.
8. Rendle, *The Multigenerational Congregation*, 138.
9. Hudson, *Evaluating Ministry*, 66.
10. Erwin Berry, *The Alban Personnel Handbook for Congregations* (Bethesda, Md.: Alban Institute, 1999).